Library Perspectives on NREN

The National Research and Education Network

EDITED BY

Carol A. Parkhurst

Library and Information Technology Association
A Division of the American Library Association
Chicago 1990

Printed on 60-pound acid-free Mohawk and bound in 10-point CIS Challenger cover by Lansing Print Shop.

The paper used in this publication meets the minimum requirements of the American National Standard for Information Sciences -- Permanence of Paper for Printed Library Materials, ANSI Z39.48-1984.

Composition, Dr. Stephen W. Wheatcraft and Carol A. Parkhurst, using Interleaf™ Technical Publishing Software; cover design, Jim Lange Design.

University of California, San Diego
Cataloging-in-Publication data:

Library perspectives on NREN : the National Research and
     Education Network / edited by Carol A. Parkhurst. --
     Chicago : Library and Information Technology
     Association, 1990.
          75 p. : ill.

          Includes bibligraphical references.
          ISBN 0-8389-7477-5

          1. National Research and Education Network (Proposed)
2. Information networks - United States. 3. Education, Higher - United States - Communication systems. I. Parkhurst, Carol A. II. Library and Information Technology Association (U.S.) III. Title: The National Research and Education Network.

LB1028.43

Contents

LITA Discussion Paper

Bibliography

Glossary

Introduction

CAROL A. PARKHURST

University of Nevada, Reno

The proposed National Research and Education Network (NREN), an electronic telecommunications infrastructure which would expand and upgrade the existing interconnected array of research networks, has become a major issue in national politics and a priority agenda item for the research and education community, libraries, government, business and industry. NREN would not only harmonize and integrate a confusing and fragmented national telecommunications networking scene, it would be built to operate at the astounding capacity of three billion bits per second by the year 2000. It is expected that the NREN would effect tremendous increases in national scientific and technological productivity by providing ready access to major supercomputing facilities and to a broad array of electronic information, and by facilitating electronic communication and collaboration among researchers and educators. The simple proposal of NREN has already served to bring about a vital and exciting discussion of access to information resources through such a network and even through existing networks.

There are many complex issues being addressed as the proposal for the NREN moves forward. Since the library community is a major stakeholder in the development of a national networking initiative, it is essential that librarians become conversant with the issues involved and that we work to influence the shape of the NREN to broadly encompass the values that we hold. The general issues are familiar:

- Open access to information

- Wide accessibility vs. availability only to an information elite

- Funding

- Commercialization

- Governance/policy–making

- Network management

- Intellectual property rights/copyright

- Privacy/data security

- User training and education

- Technical standards

Members of the Library and Information Technology Association (LITA) have taken a keen interest in the proposed NREN. The LITA Board of Directors has accepted a *Resolution on a National Research and Education Network* which was subsequently adopted by the Council of the American Library Association (ALA). The LITA Board endorses the concept of the NREN, but has taken no positions on the many issues involved in the development and use of the national network. LITA's role is an educational one: to bring information about the NREN before a broad library audience, to promote understanding of the complex issues involved, to monitor legislation, and to participate in the informal and formal coalitions that have developed and will be developed to promote the NREN.

The first major opportunity to bring the concept of the NREN to a broad library audience was during the 1990 ALA Annual Conference in Chicago. LITA presented several programs on telecommunications and networking, including the LITA President's Program, which was attended by more than 1,000 people. A *LITA Information Packet on the Proposed National Research and Education Network* was distributed at the conference; production of 2,000 NREN packets was supported by a generous donation from Innovative Interfaces, Inc. The *Packet* was so well received that the LITA Publications Committee recommended that the contents of the *Packet* be published as a monograph. The papers in the sections **NREN Legislation and Chronology, Visions of a National Network, LITA Discussion Paper,** and **Bibliography** were originally prepared for the *Packet*.

For **NREN Legislation and Chronology**, Carol C. Henderson, deputy director of the ALA Washington Office, contributed two noteworthy pieces. *National Research and Education Network Legislation S. 1067 and HR 3131: Background and Status as of September 7, 1990*, gives a clear explanation of how Federal legislation is evolving and what features are included in the major bills. *Federal Development of a National Research and Education Network: A Chronology of Significant Events and Library Community Involvement* lays out the important events which have occurred in moving the NREN concept forward, starting with legislation introduced by Senator Albert Gore, Jr. in August 1986.

The **LITA President's Program 1990: "The Promise of the Proposed National Research and Education Network (NREN) for Improved Information Access,"** was organized and moderated by Paul Evan Peters, senior program officer for technology, Association of Research Libraries. The program featured four distinguished speakers who, with little advance notice, graciously provided papers based on their presentations for inclusion in this monograph.

Dr. Vinton G. Cerf, Corporation for National Research Initiatives, accepted the challenge of *Introducing the Internet*. Dr. Cerf describes the evolution of the networks which have come to be called the Internet, and explains the governance of the computer network infrastructure in the U.S.

Dr. Charles R. McClure, in *Realizing the Promise of NREN: Social and Behavioral Considerations*, focuses on research that is being done at the School of Information Studies, Syracuse University, on social, behavioral, and policy issues related to the use of networks by researchers. Dr. McClure's paper, written with Ann Bishop, Philip Doty, and Howard Rosenbaum, is a status report on research in progress; full results will appear in a monograph to be published by Ablex in early 1991.

In *The Future of the National Research and Education Network*, Dr. John R. Garrett, Copyright Clearance Center, explores the concept of ownership of intellectual property in an electronic environment and discusses funding and control issues.

Susan K. Martin, Georgetown University, urges librarians to identify the role that they want to play in an information society. In *Libraries in the 21st Century: What We Should Do With NREN*, she speculates that librarianship might even become two professions, with those who are willing to adopt change distin-

guishing themselves from those who have a more traditional view of libraries.

To create **Visions of a National Network**, six colleagues accepted my invitation to write short papers describing visions of networking for different types of libraries and explaining innovative uses of existing networks. Craig A. Summerhill explains how electronic communications is having a profound impact on traditional methods of information gathering and dissemination in *Data Networks and the Academic Library*. Lois M. Kershner, in *A Public Library Perspective on the NREN*, advocates the need for the independent scholar to be included in the NREN through services provided by the public library. In *Electronic Networking for California State and Public Libraries*, Gary Strong, Kathy Hudson, and John Jewell describe the ways in which the State Library and public libraries in California are preparing to share their rich information resources through a national network. Steve Cisler offers a sophisticated view of *The National Research and Education Network for Special Libraries*.

To illustrate practical applications of national networking, Dr. T. M. Grundner introduces *"Free-Netting": The Development of Free, Public Access Community Computer Systems* using the Cleveland Free-Net as a prototype. In *Electronic Networking at Davis Senior High School*, Janet Meizel explains a unique partnership that has been formed among Pacific Bell, Davis Senior High School (Davis, Calif.), and the University of California, Davis to use telecommunications to support the educational process.

A **LITA Discussion Paper**, *Developing the Information Superhighway: Issues for Libraries*, was written by Dr. Edwin Brownrigg, director of research for The Memex Research Institute, at the invitation of the LITA Board. The paper is intended to provide background information and an explication of issues as a basis for ongoing discussion of library participation in the NREN. A draft of the paper was sent for review to a number of people who are prominent in the field of networking and telecommunications. Many thoughtful comments and perspectives were received, serving to illustrate that visions of the proposed NREN and of the issues involved do indeed differ, and that the opinions expressed by Dr. Brownrigg can and will be debated. Many thanks to those who took the time to share their expertise: Henriette D. Avram (Library of Congress), George

Champine (Digital Equipment Corporation), Steve Cisler (Apple Computer Library), Walt Crawford (The Research Libraries Group), Horace Flatt (IBM), Carolyn M. Gray (Brandeis University), Carol C. Henderson (ALA Washington Office), Berna L. Heyman (College of William and Mary), Thomas W. Leonhardt (University of the Pacific), Clifford Lynch (University of California), Susan K. Martin (Georgetown University), David R. McDonald (Tufts University), Jo–Ann Michalak (University of Pittsburgh), Tamara J. Miller (University of Tennessee), Paul Evan Peters (Association of Research Libraries), Nolan F. Pope (University of Wisconsin–Madison), William G. Potter (University of Georgia), Donald E. Riggs (Arizona State University), Michael M. Roberts (EDUCOM), Sherrie Schmidt (Texas A&M University), Craig A. Summerhill (Washington State University).

On behalf of the LITA Board of Directors, I would like to extend our sincere appreciation to the authors and contributors whose words and ideas follow.

Carol A. Parkhurst, assistant university librarian for systems and access services, University of Nevada, Reno, was president of LITA in 1989–90.

Resolution on a National Research and Education Network

WHEREAS, The American Library Association has followed with great interest the various legislative and administrative proposals for a National Research and Education Network; and

WHEREAS, The proposed NREN would be a high–capacity electronic highway of interconnected networks linking business, industry, government, and the education and library communities; and

WHEREAS, Libraries increasingly serve as electronic doorways to information, overcoming distance and time to deliver the totality of information resources to end users; and

WHEREAS, Libraries linked to the NREN could enhance the investment to be made in it, spread its benefits more universally, and increase access to the resources to be made available over it; now, therefore, be it

RESOLVED That the American Library Association endorse the concept of a National Research and Education Network; and, be it further

RESOLVED, That the American Library Association work to improve legislative and other proposals to increase opportunities for all types of library* participation and leadership in, and contributions to, the National Research and Education Network.

Adopted by the Council of the American Library Association, January 10, 1990

*Accepted by the LITA Board of Directors, endorsed by the LAMA Board of Directors, with the substitution of "multitype libraries" for "all types of libraries."

INTERNET
NSFNET Backbone

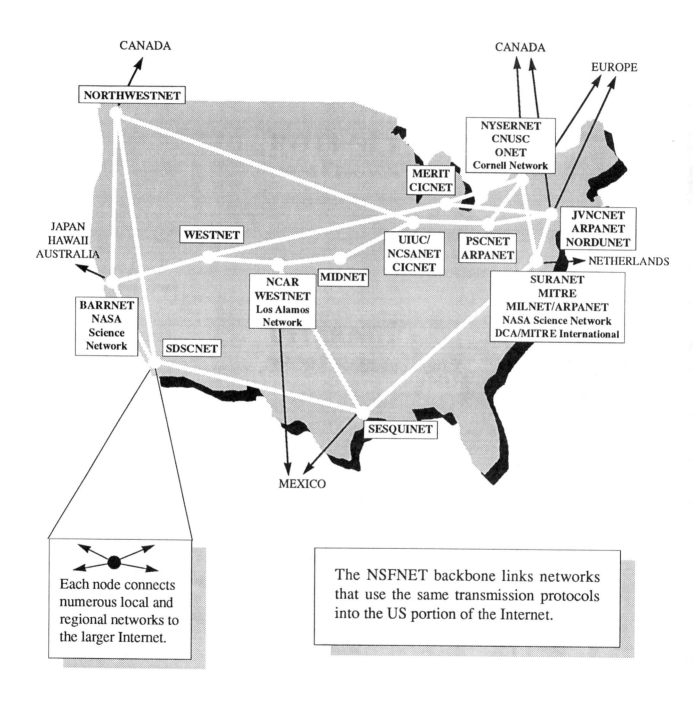

CANADA

CANADA

EUROPE

NORTHWESTNET

NYSERNET
CNUSC
ONET
Cornell Network

MERIT
CICNET

JAPAN
HAWAII
AUSTRALIA

WESTNET

JVNCNET
ARPANET
NORDUNET

UIUC/
NCSANET
CICNET

PSCNET
ARPANET

NETHERLANDS

MIDNET

NCAR
WESTNET
Los Alamos
Network

SURANET
MITRE
MILNET/ARPANET
NASA Science Network
DCA/MITRE International

BARRNET
NASA
Science
Network

SDSCNET

SESQUINET

MEXICO

Each node connects
numerous local and
regional networks to
the larger Internet.

The NSFNET backbone links networks
that use the same transmission protocols
into the US portion of the Internet.

Prepared by R. Bruce Miller and Teri Brazell,
University of California, San Diego

NREN Legislation and Chronology

National Research and Education Network Legislation S. 1067 and HR 3131

Background and Status as of June 6, 1990

CAROL C. HENDERSON

American Library Association

What is the NREN?

The proposed National Research and Education Network (or NREN, pronounced en–ren) is a telecommunications infrastructure which would expand and upgrade the existing interconnected array of mostly scientific research networks, such as the national NSFNET and regional networks such as NYSERNET and SURANET, known collectively as the Internet. The aim is to reach a 3 gigabit per second capacity by 1996, increasing current bandwidth by more than 2,000 times. A gigabit is one billion bits, and a 3 gigabit/second network could move 100,000 typed pages or 1,000 satellite photos every second.

EDUCOM, a coalition of several hundred colleges and universities promoting use of information technology in higher education, describes the goal of the NREN as:

> to enhance national competitiveness and productivity through a high speed, high quality network infrastructure which supports a broad set of applications and network services for the research and instructional community.

The concept of the NREN originated as a means to connect supercomputer centers and to accommodate the massive amounts of data produced by high performance computer projects, but such a network could accommodate other uses as well. The idea of a National Research Network gradually expanded to a National Research and Education Network, partly through the influence of EDUCOM and the Library of Congress Network Advisory Committee (composed of representatives of library associations and networks).

Establishment of the NREN is included in pending legislation as well as in the recommendations of a September 1989 report, *The Federal High Performance Computing Network*, developed by the Federal Coordinating Council for Science, Engineering, and Technology (FCCSET) and issued by President Bush's science adviser, D. Allan Bromley, director of the Office of Science and Technology Policy (OSTP).

Legislation

Legislation to establish the NREN was first introduced by Sen. Albert Gore, Jr., (D–TN) chairman of the Commerce, Science, and Transportation Subcommittee on Science, Technology, and Space, in 1988 in the 100th Congress. The National High–Performance Computer Technology Act was introduced again in 1989 as S. 1067. Rep. Doug Walgren (D–PA), then chairman of the Science, Space, and Technology Subcommittee on Science, Research, and Technology, introduced an identical bill, HR 3131. Both science subcommittees and the House telecommunications subcommittee have held hearings on the legislation.

A revised version of S. 1067 was approved by the Senate Commerce, Science, and Transportation Committee on April 3, 1990, and the Committee's report (S. Rept. 101–387) on the bill was issued on July 23. As approved, the High–Performance Computing Act of 1990 includes some of the language making library linkages more explicit, as suggested jointly by several library associations. S. 1067 contains seven titles:

TITLE I, National High–Performance Computing Plan. Coordination among federal agencies through FCCSET. Development of interagency R&D plan, including planning for the NREN. Roles defined for several science agencies, and the Department of Education and the three national libraries.

TITLE II, National Research and Education Network. National Science Foundation to work with other agencies to establish a multi–gigabit NREN by 1996 to connect computers and their users at universities, federal and industry labs, libraries, schools, and other institutions. When national commercial high–speed networks can meet the needs of researchers, the network is to be phased out. Mechanisms for charging for the use of previously published, copyrighted material available over the NREN are to be explored where feasible.

TITLE III, Information Services. NSF would be the lead agency for ensuring that federally funded databases and network services can be accessed over the NREN. Services would include directories of users, federal data banks, digital libraries of books and journals in electronic form, software libraries, and research facilities. Access to commercial information services (not now available over the Internet) would be provided, and charging mechanisms would be explored.

TITLE IV, Software. Calls for software R&D, especially for "Grand Challenge" fundamental problems in science and engineering, open software standards development, and clearinghouses for research software.

TITLE V, Computer Systems. Encourages development of new supercomputing technology by the private sector.

TITLE VI, Basic Research and Education. Science agencies would promote basic research in computer technology and for education of computer scientists, computational scientists, certain engineers, and library and information scientists.

TITLE VII, Authorizations for FY 1991–95. $338 million authorized to NASA for the purposes of the Act. To NSF: $195 million to establish the network, $64 million for basic research and education, and the remaining $391 million for the other purposes of titles III, IV, and V. The average annual cost would be $328 million, modest compared to the annual federal R&D expenditure of $70 billion.

Separate legislation (S. 1976), introduced in November 1989 by Sens. Johnston (D–LA) and McClure (R–ID) of the Energy and Natural Resources Committee, began as a bill to define and authorize the Department of Energy portion of the multi–agency program called for in S. 1067. As revised and approved by the Committee on June 27, 1990 (S. Rept. 101–377, issued July 19), the bill would

replace NSF with the Department of Education (DOE) as the agency to develop and manage the NREN.

Negotiations continue at this writing between the Senate energy and science committees on a compromise bill to combine S. 1067 and S. 1976.

In the House, a provision roughly equivalent to the title I interagency planning component of S. 1067 and HR 3131 was passed on July 11, 1990, as part of the American Technology Preeminence Act, HR 4329. This omnibus technology bill includes the National High Performance Computer Technology Program, which would require the President to submit a five–year plan to support the development of the NREN, but with no authorization of funds for this purpose. HR 4329 had been introduced in March by a majority of members of the House Science, Space, and Technology Committee. No action has been taken so far on HR 3131.

Administration Actions

High performance computing, including the development of the NREN, is one of four current Administration science priorities. (The others are education, economic competitiveness, and global change.) However, it was not identified as a priority in the President's FY 1991 budget. OSTP Director Bromley has testified at least three times in support of a high–performance computing program and the NREN, but clarifies that the Administration prefers not to have separate legislation.

In June 1990 the National Science Foundation announced that NSF and the Defense Advanced Research Projects Agency will provide $15.8 million for a three–year research project to develop the technology to enable networks and computers to support multi–gigabit/second speeds. A number of communications and high–tech companies will also make financial commitments and participate in the joint project. The research to be conducted by national laboratories, universities, supercomputer centers, and companies will be overseen by the Corporation for National Research Initiatives in Reston, Virginia, which received the grant.

Library Interest

Paul Gherman, director of libraries at Virginia Polytechnic Institute and State University, testified on March 15, 1990 at the most recent hearings on HR

3131. He represented the American Library Association and the Association of Research Libraries. His testimony concluded:

> The original vision for the NREN was to make supercomputing more broadly available to scientists and researchers. It was a very worthwhile initiative. However, I believe the vision the library community has presented to you here today sees in the NREN the possibility of transforming the very basis of scholarly communication in our nation. This vision offers a new efficiency, quality, and speed by which information can be accessed....

ALA President Richard M. Dougherty announced in his inaugural speech in June 1990 that he would devote his year as ALA President to support of a national electronic network including broad participation for all types of libraries to ensure access for all to the information resources available via this network. In March 1990, the formation of the Coalition for Networked Information (CNI) was announced by the Association of Research Libraries, CAUSE, and EDUCOM. CNI will promote the provision of information resources on existing networks and on proposed interconnected networks.

By varying estimates, there are as many as 70 library online catalogs currently available on the Internet. The Internet now connects, in addition to universities and labs, a number of undergraduate institutions, a small number of high schools, and at least one public library. Linkages from existing library networks to the NREN could help expand access beyond recipients of federal grants to smaller organizations and other students, including those distant from major research centers. Libraries of all types linked to the NREN would enhance the national investment in the network, spread its benefits more widely, and increase access to the resources available over it through an institution already established to assist users with information needs.

Revisions in the Senate committee-approved S. 1067 move in this direction. The purposes now include federal government support for making information services available over the network. The coordination among federal agencies involved in a national high-performance computing plan would now include the national libraries and the Department of Education, all of which are to encourage the distribution of library and information resources

through the NREN. Libraries and schools are to be provided access to the NREN and its resources. Network services are to include orientation and training of users. Library and information science would be added to the research and education title.

Outlook

The outlook for further movement toward the development of the NREN is good. The initiative has gathered considerable momentum and support. The question is how much movement will take place, and how quickly. It is expected that the Administration's FY 1992 budget submitted in January 1991 will devote more attention and funds to the high-performance computing program, including the NREN.

If the Senate science and energy committees can reach a compromise in combining S. 1067 and S. 1976 that is acceptable to the involved constituencies (including the education and library communities), legislation might yet make it through the process in 1990. Another possible vehicle is the House-passed technology bill, HR 4329, which could go to a House-Senate conference with a comparable Senate bill (S. 1191, which has no NREN planning provision). Once legislation is passed, funding would have to be appropriated — a separate annual, and by no means guaranteed, step.

Drafts of Senate compromise bills circulating in August 1990 had some problems, but seemed to be improving. A set of joint recommendations on S. 1067, developed by the American Library Association Washington Office, was delivered to the Senate Commerce, Science, and Transportation Committee and the Senate Energy and Natural Resources Committee on September 9, 1990. The document recommended certain changes to the joint Senate Energy-Commerce Committee staff working draft dated August 13. The recommendations were jointly sponsored by ALA, the American Association of Law Libraries, the Association of Research Libraries, the Coalition for Networked Information, the Chief Officers of State Library Agencies, EDUCOM, the Special Libraries Association, and the U.S. National Commission on Libraries and Information Science.

Conclusion

Public access to the NREN through the nation's libraries, as provided in S. 1067 as reported, could address congressional concern expressed at all the hearings that the NREN not be available only to an information elite. While many NREN implementation issues remain to be worked out, on balance, the library community sees the evolving NREN legislation as an important and positive milestone in the provision of information resources, and deserving of support. On January 10, 1990, the ALA Council passed a Resolution on a National Research and Education Network (1989–90 CD #54), endorsing the concept of the NREN and resolving to "work to improve legislative and other proposals to increase opportunities for all types of library participation and leadership in, and contributions to, the National Research and Education Network."

Prepared by Carol C. Henderson, deputy director, American Library Association Washington Office, 110 Maryland Avenue, N. E., Washington, DC 20002–5675; Phone: 202/547–4440; Fax: 202/547–7363; ALANET: ALA0025.

Federal Development of a National Research and Education Network

A Chronology of Significant Events and Library Community Involvement

CAROL C. HENDERSON

American Library Association

August 21, 1986	Legislation introduced by Senator Albert Gore, Jr., (D–TN) required the Office of Science and Technology Policy to provide Congress with an analysis of the networking needs of academic and federal research computer and supercomputer programs, and "the benefits and opportunities that an improved computer network would offer for electronic mail, file transfer, and remote access and communications for universities and Federal research facilities in the United States." The provision was enacted into law on August 21, 1986, as part of the National Science Foundation Authorization Act for FY 1987 (P.L. 99–383, 100 Stat. 816).
November 20, 1987	The Office of Science and Technology Policy (OSTP), in compliance with PL 99–383, issued *A Research and Development Strategy for High Performance Computing*, developed by the Federal Coordinating Council for Science, Engineering, and Technology (FCCSET) Committee on Computer Research and Applications. The report recommended: "U.S. government, industry, and universities should coordinate research and development for a research network to provide a distributed computing capability that links the government, industry, and higher education communities."
August 11, 1988	The Senate Commerce, Science, and Transportation Subcommittee on Science, Technology, and Space concluded hearings to examine new developments in computing and computer networking.
October 19, 1988	Sen. Gore, chairman of the Science, Technology, and Space Subcommittee, introduced S. 2918, National High–Performance Computer Technology Act of 1988. The bill included title II, National Research Computer Network, and title III, National Information Infrastructure.
December 5–7, 1988	The Library of Congress Network Advisory Committee (on which ALA is represented) held a joint meeting with EDUCOM on "Connecting the Networks" (Proceedings published in 1989 by LC as #18, *Network Planning Papers*). The proposed NREN was a major focus. The two groups agreed on a joint statement: "Our common effort must recognize our shared mission of service to the information user. These users can best be served through interconnected networks. The members of NAC and EDUCOM will work together in a coalition whose purpose is to achieve this common vision."
January, 1989	The ALA Legislation Committee was informally alerted to S. 2918 shortly after its introduction, but the NREN appeared as a formal Committee agenda item for the first time at the 1989 Midwinter Meeting. NREN developments have continued to be a regular agenda item.

May 18, 1989	Sen. Gore introduced S. 1067, the National High-Performance Computer Technology Act of 1989, an updated version of S. 2918 from the previous Congress. Title II was revised and called the National Research and Education Network. In introductory remarks, Sen. Gore said: "Libraries, rural schools, minority institutions, and vocational education programs will have access to the same national resources -- data bases, supercomputers, accelerators -- as more affluent and better known institutions" (May 18, 1989, *Congressional Record*, p. S5689). He envisioned the National Information Infrastructure of title III as a "National Digital Library."
June, 1989	The ALA Washington Office began coverage of legislation to establish the NREN in the *ALA Washington Newsletter* and the *Legislative Report of the ALA Washington Office* (distributed widely at ALA conferences, including to ALA Council). Coverage continues regularly in these publications as well as in the *ALA Washington Newsline* on the ALANET electronic mail system.
June 21, 1989 July 26, 1989	The Senate Commerce, Science, and Transportation Subcommittee on Science, Technology, and Space held hearings on S. 1067.
August 3, 1989	Rep. Doug Walgren (D-PA), then chairman of the Science, Research and Technology Subcommittee, and ranking minority member Sherwood Boehlert (R-NY); Rep. Robert Roe (D-NY), chairman of the parent Science, Space, and Technology Committee; and several other members introduced HR 3131, the National High-Performance Computer Technology Act of 1989, an identical companion measure to S. 1067.
September, 1989	The congressional Office for Technology Assessment issued *High Performance Computing and Networking for Science -- Background Paper* (OTA-BP-CIT-59, GPO), with a detailed discussion of NREN issues.
September 8, 1989	D. Allan Bromley, President Bush's new science advisor and director of the Office of Science and Technology Policy, issued a development plan for the NREN in *The Federal High Performance Computing Program*. The report was written by representatives of more than a dozen agencies working with OSTP. "Education" was included in the name of the network in explicit recognition of the importance of the inter-relationships between the network, research, and education, according to this report. At congressional hearings on September 15, Dr. Bromley testified that the Administration preferred to address this high-priority initiative through administrative action rather than through separate legislation.
September 15, 1989	The Senate Commerce, Science, and Transportation Subcommittee on Science, Technology, and Space held hearings on S. 1067. Witnesses included Librarian of Congress James Billington accompanied by Henriette Avram, LC assistant librarian for processing services; and Daniel Masys, director of Lister Hill National Center for Biomedical Communications, National Library of Medicine. Dr. Billington said that high-capacity data networks could allow LC to become a "library without walls," providing scholars nationwide with access to its materials, and expanding far beyond its traditional role of providing bibliographic information.
October 3, 1989	The House Science, Space, and Technology Subcommittee on Science, Research, and Technology held a hearing on High Performance Computing, including the NREN.
October 4, 1989	The House Energy and Commerce Subcommittee on Telecommunications and Finance held a hearing on the nation's telecommunications infrastructure and the "network of the future." Subcommittee chairman Edward Markey (D-MA) is a cosponsor of HR 3131.

November 21, 1989	Sen. J. Bennett Johnston (D–LA) and Sen. James McClure (R–ID), chairman and ranking minority member of the Energy and Natural Resources Committee, and Sen. Albert Gore, Jr., introduced S. 1976, the Department of Energy High–Performance Computing Act of 1989. S. 1976 would define and authorize the DOE portion of the multi–agency program proposed in S. 1067.
January 9, 1990	The National Telecommunications and Information Administration (NTIA) in the Commerce Department initiated a study of the domestic telecommunications infrastructure (55 *Federal Register* 800–818). The numerous issues on which NTIA sought public comment included the NREN.
January 10, 1990	The American Library Association Council passed a Resolution on a National Research and Education Network (1989–90 CD #54), endorsing the concept of the NREN and resolving to "work to improve legislative and other proposals to increase opportunities for all types of library participation and leadership in, and contributions to, the National Research and Education Network." The resolution originated with ALA's Library and Information Technology Association.
February 1, 1990	A cooperative library working group led by Jim Benn of NCLIS and Carol Henderson of the ALA Washington Office drafted proposed amendments to the ongoing Senate staff revision of S. 1067. Library organizations represented included the American Library Association, the Association of Research Libraries, the Chief Officers of State Library Agencies, the Special Libraries Association, and the U. S. National Commission on Libraries and Information Science. The amendments and supporting rationale, designed to strengthen library linkages to the NREN, were discussed with staff of the Senate Science, Technology, and Space Subcommittee on February 1. Most of these suggestions were incorporated into the revised bill subsequently approved by the parent Commerce, Science, and Transportation Committee. The amendments were also discussed with House subcommittee staff.
March 6, 1990	The Senate Energy and Natural Resources Subcommittee on Energy Research and Development held hearings on S. 1976.
March 14–15, 1990	The House Science, Space, and Technology Subcommittee on Science, Research, and Technology held hearings on HR 3131. On March 15, Paul Gherman, Director of Libraries at Virginia Polytechnic Institute and State University, testified in support of HR 3131 on behalf of the American Library Association and the Association of Research Libraries.
March 15, 1990	Sen. Gore's keynote speech on the NREN introduced the National Net '90 Conference, the third annual meeting organized by EDUCOM and cosponsoring groups to forge a strategic partnership among education, government and industry in pursuit of the NREN. A library session on "Information Resources and the National Network" was organized by the Association of Research Libraries Telecommunications Task Force.
March 16, 1990	The formation of the Coalition for Networked Information was announced by the Association of Research Libraries, CAUSE, and EDUCOM. CNI will promote the provision of information resources on existing networks and on proposed interconnected networks.
March 21, 1990	D. Allan Bromley, the President's science advisor and director of OSTP, addressed the Forum on Federal Information Policies, sponsored by the Federal Library and Information Center Committee at the Library of Congress. He listed four current priorities for OSTP: education, economic competitiveness, global change, and high–performance computing,

the last to include building the NREN. He said: "Imagine how the role of libraries will change when most American homes are connected to them over local networks via a wide-bandwidth channel....Individuals would be able to search their local library or other repositories electronically to select and retrieve text and pictures, rent and view a movie, or research specific needs...all of these are technically feasible today."

March 21, 1990	Chairman Robert Roe, ranking minority member Robert Walker (R–PA), Rep. Tim Valentine (who had just days before become chairman of the Science, Research, and Technology Subcommittee), and a majority of members of the Science, Space, and Technology Committee introduced HR 4329, the American Technology Preeminence Act. The Committee approved the bill the same day and issued its report (H. Rept. 101–481, Part I) on May 10, when HR 4329 was referred to the Judiciary Committee. This omnibus technology bill includes as title VII, the National High Performance Computer Technology Program, the plan for which is to include establishment of the NREN. HR 4329 would incorporate elements of HR 3131, but without any specific authorization of funds.
April 3, 1990	S. 1067 was ordered favorably reported by the Senate Commerce, Science, and Transportation Committee with an amendment in the nature of a substitute, which included a number of library community recommendations. The Committee's report on S. 1067 was issued on July 23.
April 5, 1990	The ALA Washington Office submitted comments on behalf of ALA in response to NTIA's notice of inquiry and request for comments on a Comprehensive Study of Domestic Telecommunications Infrastructure. ALA recommended support of NREN development with public access through the nation's libraries. Representatives of several ALA units reviewed a draft of the ALA comments.
April 24, 1990	Sen. Gore spoke about S. 1067 and his vision of the NREN at the morning briefing for participants at the 16th Annual National Library Week Legislative Day, sponsored by the American Library Association, the D. C. Library Association, and the Special Libraries Association. Briefing materials prepared by the ALA Washington Office included background and status information on NREN legislation. More than 550 library supporters from 48 states and D. C. visited congressional offices to discuss library issues, including S. 1067 and HR 3131.
May 10, 1990	The House Science, Space, and Technology Committee issued its report (H. Rept. 101–481) on HR 4329, the American Technology Preeminence Act, which incorporates the NREN interagency planning element.
June, 1990	The Library and Information Technology Association, a division of ALA, issued *LITA Information Packet on the Proposed National Research and Education Network*, to bring information about the NREN before a broad library audience.
June 8, 1990	The National Science Foundation announced that NSF and the Defense Advanced Research Projects Agency will provide $15.8 million for a three–year research project to develop the technology to enable networks and computers to support multi–gigabit/second speeds. A number of communications and high-tech companies will also make financial commitments and participate in the joint project. The research to be conducted by national laboratories, universities, supercomputer centers, and companies will be overseen by the Corporation for National Research Initiatives in Reston, Virginia, which received the grant.

June 27, 1990	The Senate Energy and Natural Resources Committee ordered reported S. 1976, the Department of Energy High–Performance Computing Act of 1990, with a substitute amendment.
June 27, 1990	Richard M. Dougherty, in his inaugural speech as ALA President, said that the debate now underway about how the national electronic network should look and whom it should serve is "one in which we as librarians have a national responsibility to participate." He pledged to devote his year as ALA President to support of "a national electronic network that serves all of us, that serves the democratic aims of our society, that empowers the citizenry in the ways that only information literacy can empower."
July, 1990	The Association of Research Libraries issued *Linking Researchers and Resources: The Emerging Information Infrastructure and the NREN Proposal* (ARL Briefing Package No. 4).
July 11, 1990	The House by a vote of 327–93 passed a revised version of the American Technology Pre-eminence Act. Section 402 of HR 4329 includes the National High Performance Computer Technology Program, which would require the President to submit a five–year plan to support the development of the NREN. The bill contains no authorization of funds for the NREN.
July 15, 1990	In "Networking the Future," in the *Washington Post*, Sen. Gore described the high–capacity information network as the "on–ramp to tomorrow," needed to make the most of high-performance computers. "If we had the information superhighways we need, a school child could plug into the Library of Congress...and explore a universe of knowledge...." For a lay audience, Sen. Gore's article underscored his broad vision for the NREN and its far-reaching implications. It was inserted in the July 16 *Congressional Record*, pp. S9762–63.
July 19, 1990	The Senate Energy and Natural Resources Committee issued its report (S. Rept. 101–377) on S. 1976, the Department of Energy High–Performance Computing Act of 1990. As (rather unexpectedly) revised by the Committee, the bill would replace NSF with the Department of Education (DOE) as the agency to develop and manage the NREN, with users expected to include industry, the higher education community, researchers, librarians, federal agencies, and information service providers. Negotiations began between the Senate energy and science committees on a compromise bill to combine S. 1067 and S. 1976.
July 23, 1990	The Senate Commerce, Science, and Transportation Committee issued its report (S. Rept. 101–387) on S. 1067 as revised and approved by the Committee on April 3. Among the revisions approved by the Committee: Purposes now include federal support for making information services available over the network. Coordination among federal agencies involved in a national high–performance computing plan would include the Department of Education, the Library of Congress, the National Agricultural Library, and the National Library of Medicine, all of which are to encourage the distribution of library and information resources through the NREN. Libraries and schools are to be provided access to the NREN and its resources. Network services are to include orientation and training of users. Library and information science would be added to the research and education title.
September 5, 1990	A set of joint recommendations on S. 1067, developed by the American Library Association Washington Office, was delivered to the Senate Commerce, Science, and Transportation Committee and the Senate Energy and Natural Resources Committee. The document recommended certain changes to the joint Senate Energy–Commerce Committee staff working draft dated August 13. The recommendations were jointly sponsored by ALA and the American Association of Law Libraries, the Association of Research Libraries, the

Coalition for Networked Information, the Chief Officers of State Library Agencies, EDU-COM, the Special Libraries Association, and the U. S. National Commission on Libraries and Information Science.

Prepared by Carol C. Henderson, deputy director, American Library Association Washington Office, 110 Maryland Avenue, N. E., Washington, DC 20002–5675; Phone: 202/547–4440; Fax: 202/547–7363; ALANET: ALA0025.

LITA President's Program 1990

The Promise of the Proposed
National Research and Education Network
for Improved Information Access

Introducing the Internet

Dr. Vinton G. Cerf

Corporation for National Research Initiatives

The Internet is an international collaboration of more than 5,000 computer networks in 35 countries serving over one million researchers and scholars in universities, government research facilities, and private industrial laboratories working in many different disciplines.

The system began as a research project on the interconnection of packet communication networks sponsored by the U.S. Defense Advanced Research Projects Agency (DARPA) and now has the support of many U.S. government agencies as well as other international organizations in the government, academic and business sectors.

The evolution of this system (particularly its protocols and architecture) is overseen by a volunteer Internet Activities Board (IAB) which has subsidiary organizations to carry out its work: the Internet Engineering Task Force (IETF) and the Internet Research Task Force (IRTF). The evolution of the IAB/IETF/IRTF is illustrated in Figure 1.

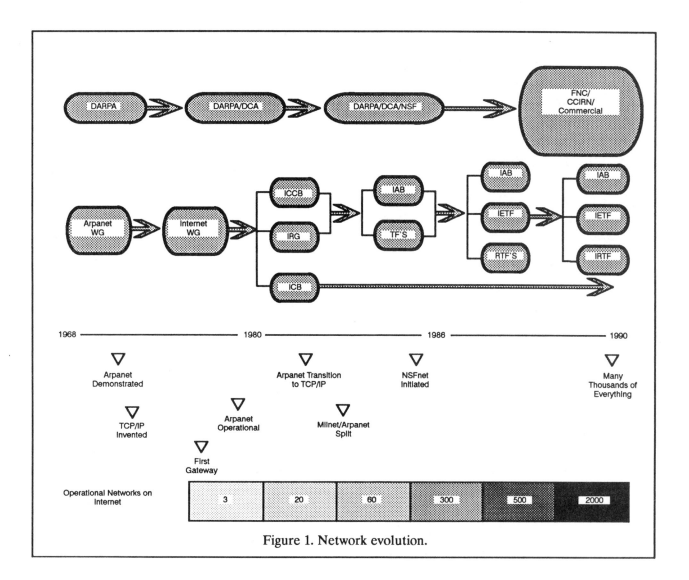

Figure 1. Network evolution.

Definitions for the acronyms used in Figure 1:

ARPA — Advanced Research Projects Agency (old name for DARPA)

ARPANET — The first packet network in the Internet.

CCIRN — Coordinating Committee for Intercontinental Research Networking. Cochaired by the FNC Executive Director and the RARE Executive Director.

DARPA — Defense Advanced Research Projects Agency

DCA — Defense Communications Agency; operator of the Defense Data Network (DDN) and supporter of the Network Information Center (NIC) at SRI International.

FNC — Federal Networking Council; joint U.S. Government body which oversees U.S. federal policy on networking.

ICB — International Coordination Board; coordinates actions among NATO and other military members of the Internet.

ICCB — Internet Configuration Control Board; early predecessor to the IAB.

IESG — Internet Engineering Steering Group; made up of chairmen of eight areas into which IETF work is divided. Makes recommendations on standards to the Internet Activities Board.

IETF — Internet Engineering Task Force; responsible for day to day evolution of the Internet System and for immediate protocol specification problem resolution. Also has some operational coordination responsibility. Standardization of the Internet protocol suite takes place largely within IETF.

IP — Internet Protocol; used to move packets among host computers and through gateways if necessary.

IRTF — Internet Research Task Force; made up of chairmen of several Internet research groups. Responsible for helping to organize longer–term research and protocol development for the Internet.

MILNET — Military packet network; part of the Defense Data Net and user of the ARPANET technology.

NSF — National Science Foundation; founder of the NSFNET. Provides mainstay support for a broad range of research work in the U.S.

RARE — Reseaux Associees Recherche d'Europeene (Association of European Research Networks).

RFC — Request for Comment; also called an "RFC", a Request for Comment is one of a series of nearly 1,200 such documents, some of which document protocols, others of which merely inform.

TCP — Transmission Control Protocol; end to end protocol which assures reliable, sequenced delivery of data.

TCP/IP — Term used to refer to the Internet protocol suite, named after the two primary protocols: TCP and IP.

A more complete outline of the Internet Activities Board and its operation may be found in *Request for Comment 1160*, published through SRI International, 333 Ravenswood Drive, Menlo Park, CA 94025. The document may be obtained by ordering from the Network Information Center (NIC) at SRI International.

Networks on the Internet

There are many networks which make up the Internet. A list of a few of the 5,000 systems is given in Figure 2. A more complete (but still not totally complete) summary of these systems can be found in *The Matrix* by John S. Quarterman, published in 1990 by Digital Press. The Internet chapter begins on page 277.

Statistics

Nearly 5,000 networks have been assigned network numbers and are potentially connected to the Internet. Another 13,000 networks have been assigned numbers but plan to operate privately and not to connect to the rest of the system. Of the 5,000 which may connect, approximately 2,000 of them are online and being serviced by the NSFNET and other backbones; the remainder are expected to interlink soon.

Backbone Nets

NSFNET – National Science Foundation Network

HEPNET – High Energy Physics Network

NSINET – NASA Science Internet

DRINET – Defense Research Internet

DDN/MILNET – Defense Data Network/Military Network

ESNET – Energy Sciences Network

ARPANET – Advanced Research Projects Agency Network (retired)

European Nets

JANET – Joint Academic Network (UK)

EARN – European Academic Research Network

FNET – French Research Network

SURFNET – Belgian University Network

IXI – International eXchange Internet

DFNET – German Research Network

Figure 2. Sample of networks on Internet.

As of May 1990, the NSFNET was passing 3.15 billion packets per month. At the end of August 1990, this number had risen to about 3.7 billion packets per month. The traffic on the NSFNET, which is representative of traffic throughout the Internet, is split between interactive applications (18%), electronic mail (27%), file transfers (28%), domain name lookup (10%) and other services (17%). Figures 3, 4 and 5 illustrate patterns of usage of the NSFNET.

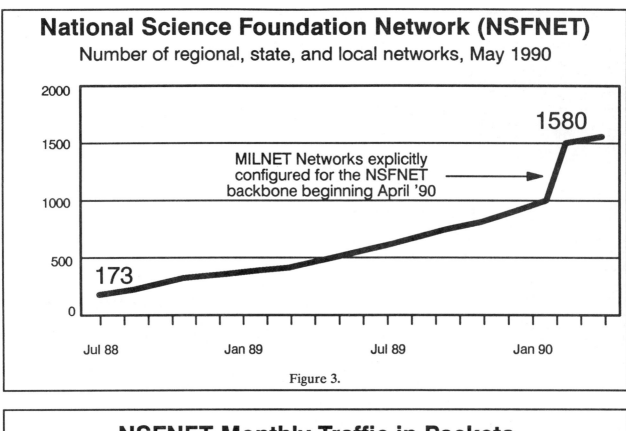

National Science Foundation Network (NSFNET)
Number of regional, state, and local networks, May 1990

1580

MILNET Networks explicitly
configured for the NSFNET
backbone beginning April '90

173

Jul 88   Jan 89   Jul 89   Jan 90

Figure 3.

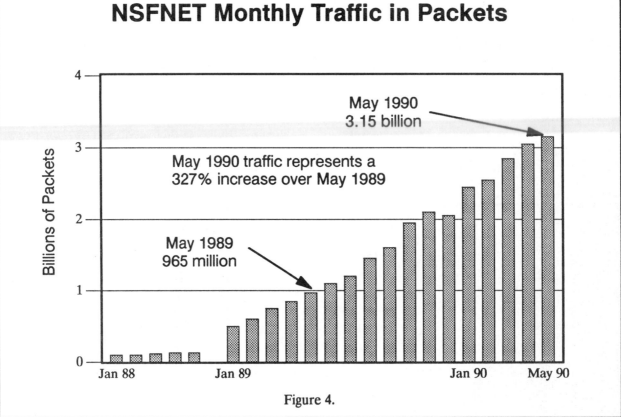

NSFNET Monthly Traffic in Packets

May 1990
3.15 billion

May 1990 traffic represents a
327% increase over May 1989

May 1989
965 million

Jan 88   Jan 89   Jan 90   May 90

Figure 4.

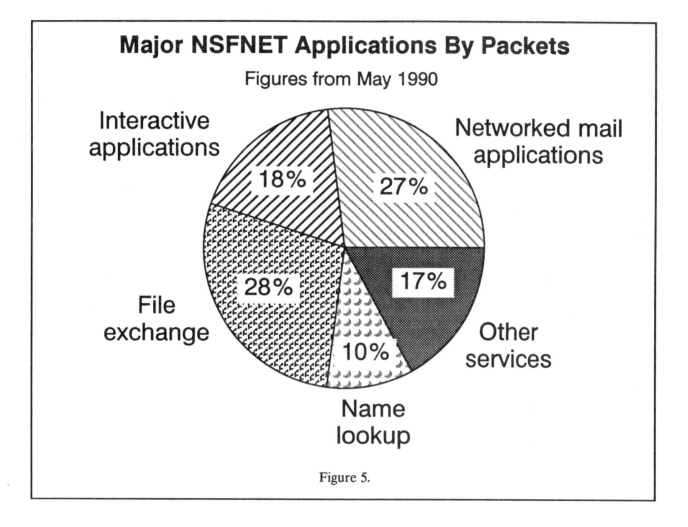

Figure 5.

The Federal Networking Council (FNC)

Formed in 1990 under the sponsorship of the Office of Science and Technology Policy (OSTP) which is headed by the President's science advisor (Dr. D. Allan Bromley), the Federal Networking Council is responsible for organizing and coordinating Federal involvement in the development and provision of a computer network infrastructure in the U.S. The present chairman of the FNC is Dr. Charles Brownstein, who is also acting director of the Computer, Information Sciences and Engineering directorate of the National Science Foundation.

CISE
National Science Foundation
1800 G Street, N.W. Washington, D.C. 20550

email: CBrownst@nsf.gov
tel: (202) 357-7936

Figures 6, 7, and 8 illustrate aspects of the Federal Networking Council (FNC) and the FNC Advisory Committee.

Federal Networking Council

- FORMED BY FCCSET/Network SubCommittee Chair (JAN. 4, 90)

- PURPOSES

    – Provide [Federal] Policy Direction for NREN Vision
    – Coordinate Activities and Services of Federal Nets
    – Establish Mechanisms to Ensure Inter–Operation

- I.E. – FNC WAS FORMED TO ESTABLISH AN INTERAGENCY FORUM AND LONG TERM STRATEGY TO OVERSEE THE OPERATION AND EVOLUTION OF THE INTERNET.

- MEMBERS FORMALLY DESIGNATED BY THEIR AGENCIES

    If NREN is Funded, the Internet Will Evolve to NREN

Figure 6.

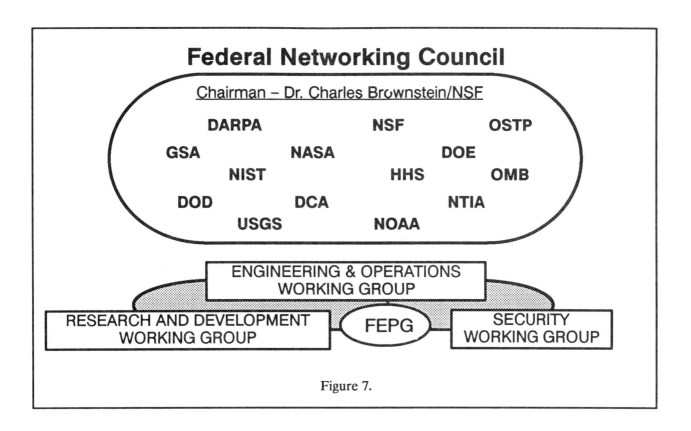

Figure 7.

FNC Advisory Committee

FNC, coordinating with the Office of Science and Technology Policy, will establish a charter and formal Advisory Committee representing industry and academia and the national user community; this Advisory Committee will work closely with the FNC to provide guidance in developing the NREN.

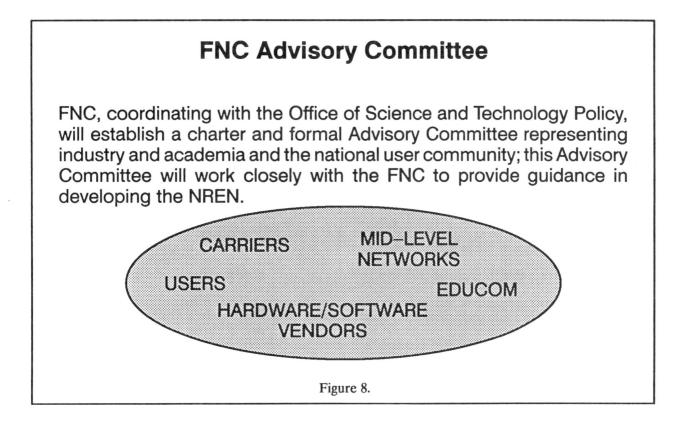

Figure 8.

Principal Foci for Internet Evolution: 1990–1991

Operational Stability

- Internet Instrumentation (Fault Isolation, Data Gathering and Analysis)

- Open Internal Gateway Protocol

- Domain Name Server/Resolver Repair

- Inter–Autonomous Region Routing

- Topology Management

User Services

- White Pages/Knowbot Information Services

- Private Electronic Mail

- Public, Private, International E-mail Links

- Application Support Tools/Protocols

OSI Integration

- Multiprotocol Gateways

- X.400/RFC 822 Relays

- X.500 Pilot Projects

- Registration Facilities

Testbed Facilities

- Terrestrial Wideband Conferencing/Collaboration Research

- Multivendor Gateway Testing: Network Management, and Multiprotocol routing/forwarding

- Open Architecture Gateway Testbed for new ETE Protocols

Getting Big

- Large Scale Internet Architectures

- Naming, Addressing, Routing, Navigation

Getting Fast

- Limits to Internet Architecture?

- High Speeds and Latency

- Internet Use of Gigabit Technology

Applications

- Digital Library Services

- Transaction Processing

- Video Conferencing

- Security Services

For More Information

- To be added to the IETF mailing list or for general information requests:
  IETF-REQUEST@ISI.EDU

- For protocol advancement or other specific information questions:
  IESG-SECRETARY@NRI.RESTON.VA.US

- To order copies of the IETF Proceedings:
  PROCEEDINGS@NRI.RESTON.VA.US

- To submit Internet-Draft documents or to get information about I–Ds:
  INTERNET-DRAFTS@NRI.RESTON.VA.US

Dr. Vinton G. Cerf is vice–president, Corporation for National Research Initiatives and chair of the Internet Activities Board.

Realizing the Promise of the NREN: Social and Behavioral Considerations

A Status Report on a Study in Progress

DR. CHARLES R. MCCLURE, ANN BISHOP, PHILIP DOTY AND HOWARD ROSENBAUM

School of Information Studies
Syracuse University

Introduction

Much attention has been devoted recently to the Federal government's plans for the development of a high–speed "national research and education network" (NREN). Such a network is envisioned as an electronic highway connecting researchers to each other and to computerized research tools. Because many research efforts rely on collaboration and are becoming increasingly interdisciplinary, geographically dispersed researchers frequently need to be able to communicate quickly and easily. The current system of electronic networks appears inadequate: networks are not standardized, and many are in danger of being overwhelmed by the number of users they support and the amount of information they transmit. An enhanced national research network would support the more effective use of scientific resources and personnel.

In May of 1989, Senator Albert Gore of Tennessee introduced S. 1067, the "National High–Performance Computer Technology Act of 1989." A nearly identical bill, H.R. 3131, was introduced in the House by Congressman Doug Walgren. The proposed legislation defines the government's role in high–performance computing and authorizes the funding and creation of a high–capacity electronic research and education network to link the national supercomputer centers, educational institutions, and other research and development facilities throughout

Portions of this study have been supported by the U.S. Congress, Office of Technology Assessment, under contract no. L3–2225.0.

Full results will appear in a monograph by the authors, tentatively titled *Electronic Networks, the Research Process, and Scholarly Communication*, to be published in early 1991 by Ablex.

the United States. In the Executive branch, the Office of Science and Technology Policy has produced two reports that describe a broad national agenda for the development of advanced information technologies and delineate a plan for the implementation of a national research and education network.

The government's rationale for this investment rests on projected increases in the efficiency of and return on investment from R&D in the United States and on anticipated improvements in technology transfer. The ultimate aim is to improve national competitiveness and the national welfare. Much as the interstate highway system was an investment in the nation's transportation infrastructure, the investment in a national research network hopes to realize similar, widespread national benefits by improving the country's information technology infrastructure.

Most government initiatives related to NREN focus on resolving technical problems and issues, giving little or no attention to social and behavioral issues that will have an important impact on the eventual adoption and use of the network. Expanding on the highway metaphor, Robert Kahn, president of the Corporation for National Research Initiatives, notes the need for attention to such non–technical issues as assuring universal access and developing user support services and effective policies; he warns that the information highway involves "more than just laying down concrete. We need the connecting roads, the highway services, and the transportation functions." The needed policies and user services should be based on an understanding of researchers' patterns of communication and information seeking and use. There is little empirical evidence, however, about how many researchers are regular users of the existing national network structure, what the vast majority of researchers use networks for, and about how the networks affect their work. Few investigations have focused on the problems faced by both "high profile" and other users of electronic research networks, or on how researchers are trained to use networks. In addition, little research has been done on major policy issues related to the design and implementation of a national research network.

Study Objective and Approach

Over the past two years, we have been investigating social, behavioral, and policy issues related to the development of NREN. The aim of our work has been to:

- Describe the impact of existing networks on the research process and scientific communication

- Provide a user–perspective on network issues and applications

- Offer recommendations to increase the effectiveness of the NREN.

Our approach to the study of the NREN combined the following three techniques:

- Literature Review and Policy Analysis

- User Study
  - Focus Group Interviews
  - Individual Interviews
  - BITNET Survey
  - Questionnaire to Network Consultants

- Development of Issue Brief and Recommendations.

Assessment of Literature and Policy Instruments

The purpose of the literature review and policy analysis was to critically examine current literature and policy instruments that impact upon development and implementation of the NREN. This was done to clarify the range of key policy issues considered important by the major stakeholders, both inside and outside of the Federal government, and to mark off the boundaries of the current debate over the NREN. The review and analysis identified a number of themes or issues that are present in key policy instruments and in recent writings about the NREN.

The literature review and policy analysis focused on a broad range of materials from the open literature and eleven reports prepared or commissioned by governmental agencies, nine key pieces of legislation (one passed, one pending in the House, two pending in the Senate, and five which did not become law, but which influenced later legislation), and seven Congressional hearings, three held by House Subcommittees and four held by Senate Subcommittees.

We found that current literature and policy statements, which often extol the many virtues of a NREN, are incomplete in that they:

- Rarely examine users' problems and frustrations

- Assume universal access and connectivity

- Inadequately consider training, education, and retraining issues

- Make large claims about the universal and positive effects of information technology, i.e., exhibit "technophoria"

- Collect few data designed to give an overall national picture of the uses and effects of high–speed electronic networks

- Rarely analyze policy issues and behavioral factors attendant to a national research network initiative

- Inadequately consider the potential roles of libraries in such a network

- Assume past experience with networks have prepared policymakers, network managers, and users to deal with issues and problems from a true, integrated, multi–purpose national network.

In short, there is little empirical evidence that describes specifically how scholarly productivity has been or would be improved nationally as a result of such networks or how institutional and individual characteristics impede or encourage the successful use of electronic networks by researchers. This kind of evidence must be brought to bear on the design of the NREN.

Study of Network Users

Much of the existing literature on the impact of networks on the research process and scholarly communication ignores the fact that many researchers lack the skills, training, interest, or access to technology and other resources to take full advantage of electronic networks. The assumption that most researchers will become enthusiastic, sophisticated, and habitual users of such networks merits investigation. Similarly, claims that networks will achieve the wider and more democratic distribution of research resources also require greater attention.

Therefore, we undertook an empirical investigation of the use of electronic networks by researchers. The importance of this study lies in its investigation of these often untested claims and assumptions and its linkage of the evidence gathered from network users with analysis of major policy issues involved in the planning and implementation of a national research and education network. It represents one part of a small, but growing, effort toward assessing the significance of electronic networks for scholarly communication and research and toward considering policy strategies to promote the most effective and beneficial utilization of these networks.

Our study took a user perspective in addressing four general research questions:

1) Are claims that network technology changes the modus operandi of researchers correct?

2) What evidence exists that networks have changed basic patterns of scientific communication?

3) What problems or issues do network users face?

4) What implications do answers to these questions hold for the design and operation of a national network?

The research questions guiding the study suggested a two–phased methodological approach: (1) obtaining descriptive information (with surveys, questionnaires, interviews, and focus groups) about network uses and features and the impacts of networks on scientific research and communication, and (2) analyzing that descriptive information in light of various policy issues.

Multiple data collection techniques were used to provide information about the perceptions and experiences of research network users (both basic and advanced) and managers in academia, industry, and Federal laboratories. While such settings have obvious similarities, the study team anticipated that each setting might also exhibit different network configurations and features, concern itself with different issues, and be subject to different barriers to successful network implementation and use. One of the most difficult tasks in the development and implementation of a national network will be balancing the interests and concerns of these three major constituencies.

Within these three settings, data on the experiences and perceptions of several different populations are important: researchers who exhibit intensive use of networks, researchers who exhibit less intensive use of networks, and network managers. In order to examine the current and potential impact of research networks on scientific communication and productivity, both seasoned and novice network users were studied. Discussions with novice users served to balance the seasoned users' claims and provided important clues to the barriers faced by researchers in the use of networks. Network managers were included in the study because they are an important source of descriptive data about network features, policies, management issues, and barriers to use. They also provided important information about trends in the evolution of research networks.

Most of the data collected were qualitative. Such qualitative data were collected for several reasons. First, high–speed communication networks are relatively new, and users' behavior and needs patterns have not yet been firmly established, making traditional user studies inappropriate. Qualitative data are also useful for elucidating the meaning that a new technology has for a given community. In addition, anecdotal evidence is traditionally used in the context of policy analysis to give policy makers a better understanding of the views of particular stakeholder groups.

Network Problems and Issues

A range of problems and barriers which currently prevent the effective use of electronic networks were identified by network users, managers, and intermediaries:

• INADEQUATE EDUCATION AND TRAINING. Regardless of organizational setting, there is inadequate support for education and training of network users. Most users report that the knowledge necessary for using the network came from working with a colleague or "gutting it out" with a manual.

- LACK OF TECHNICAL STANDARDS. A major stumbling block for many users is the number of often conflicting protocols, commands, and procedures which must be understood if networks are to be used effectively. The lack of standards is compounded when users must work with different types of hardware and software.

- COMPLEX OR UNKNOWN PROCEDURES. A frequent complaint from network users is that network managers or consultants indicate that a certain procedure, e.g., uploading a dataset to transmit over the network, is a very straight–forward process. While the process may be straight–forward for a network manager or consultant, this task is often perceived as too complex and burdensome by users.

- INSUFFICIENT OR UNEVEN NETWORK CAPACITY. A relatively small number of users commented that insufficient capacity, limited speed, or need for large bandwidths was a barrier for network use. Typically, such users were high profile users who had very sophisticated computing needs.

- UNRELIABILITY OF DATA TRANSMISSION OR DATA TRANSFORMATIONS. Users commented that transmission of data that require uploading or downloading, working with different kinds of application software, or similar procedures is likely to require significant editing and review after transmission. This problem is especially bothersome to naive network users who want only to download a text file and convert it into a particular wordprocessing format.

- LACK OF USER–BASED SYSTEMS AND APPLICATIONS. The findings suggest that there is ineffective communication between network designers and managers and between these groups and network users. What network managers consider to be "user–based" system designs and procedures or "user–friendly" applications fre-

quently are not considered as such by network users.

- POOR DOCUMENTATION. Other problems mentioned frequently by users are that (1) needed documentation may not be easily available, (2) documentation is frequently not "user friendly" and requires someone else to interpret it, and (3) the rapidly changing nature of networks requires constant updating of documentation. Users noted that online documentation was of little use when the procedures for obtaining that documentation were unclear, hard to obtain, or unknown.

- INADEQUATE DIRECTORIES. Descriptive information about available network services is inadequate and there are few listings of individuals' email addresses. Users cannot make effective use of networks when they are unaware of the services that are available or are unable to contact others easily and reliably.

- INSUFFICIENT CONNECTIVITY. A major problem facing network users is connectivity among the various national networks and, oftentimes, within a single network. Some spoke of endless difficulties when attempting to send information from one network to another. Currently, connectivity among the networks is not well developed enough to be transparent to most users. On the other hand, extremely sophisticated users do not want system transparency for a number of reasons. For example, as one of the high profile users put it: "If a [technical] problem occurs, how do you discover where it is, who's responsible for it, who fixes it and who pays for fixing it?"

- TECHNOLOGICAL OVERKILL. For some users, rapid change in information technologies is, in and of itself, a barrier to effective network use. A number of users commented that more technology and more applications are counterproductive when the users are unable to use and understand the technology and applications they currently have.

- UNCERTAINTIES ABOUT NETWORK MANAGEMENT. For a number of situations, the policies and procedures that govern appropriate uses of the network are unclear or simply not available. Users are unsure who or what has responsibility for particular types of network management tasks and from whom they should seek assistance in using networks.

- DOUBTS ABOUT DATA SECURITY. Due perhaps to recent court cases involving public access to data files or back-up tapes of electronic mail, there is some question about the degree to which individuals can be confident that (1) their electronic data are secure, (2) unknown back-up systems that maintain copies of data will not be made public without consent, or (3) proprietary information will not "escape" from an organization onto the network.

All of these barriers combine to present a mosaic of problems that may limit the usefulness and effectiveness of electronic networks.

Based on the comments offered by study participants, the study team identified a number of underlying issue areas related to the design, implementation, and management of a national research network. These issue areas are important because of:

- Their overarching effects on the adoption and use of networks by researchers

- The failure of managers, network administrators, and systems analysts to recognize and address them in the design, implementation, and support of networks and related technologies

- Their relative neglect by policymakers and commentators.

Social and policy issues are in some ways more intractable than technical ones, but steps can be taken to understand and resolve them. Their interrelationships make them difficult to assess and analyze individually, and they are discussed as separate areas here only to aid comprehension and analysis.

Key Issue 1: Education, Training, and Support

It appears that a large proportion of the researchers at the sites we visited are not aware of the existence or capabilities of existing networks, do not take full advantage of networks, do not know how to use desired network functions, or do not use networks at all. One major reason for this situation seems to be the lack of formal training and adequate user technical support at the institutional level. The study's findings indicate that this situation is common

to all sectors and cuts across individual levels of expertise.

Improvement in the extent, level, and effectiveness of network education, training, and support is critical for leveraging the investment in a national network. Currently, the number of network users and the ability of researchers to exploit networks in their work are severely limited by the lack of adequate attention to these areas.

Key Issue 2: Scientific and Social Norms

Networks may prove dysfuntional to the scientific enterprise if network policies and practices do not fit into that prevailing social structure. The way researchers use networks and the way they envision network policies are influenced by prevailing scientific and social norms. Further, the norms of the research community seem to vary somewhat according to the organizational goals and constraints associated with each of the three major sectors (private, governmental, and academic).

Researchers in all sectors contended, either explicitly or implicitly, that network use is governed by, and must support, the traditional scientific norms of **communality** (free communication of ideas), **organized skepticism** (testing others' research results), **disinterestedness** (evaluating research on the basis of its intrinsic merit), and **universalism** (ignoring origin in the evaluation of research).

For example, researchers were appalled by the notion that a "competitive advantage" resulted from network access to information and other resources, by the suggestion that their network communication might be censored, and by the use of networks to circumvent the usual "quality control" and peer review processes of research. Also, reputation, publication, and reward are inextricably interwoven in the scientific community. Norms may profoundly affect network behavior, and, at the same time, networks may not be subsumable into extant norms. Current intellectual property laws and scientific reward structures may be significantly challenged if the NREN is fully developed.

Key Issue 3: Generation, Occupation, and Situation Gaps

Gaps in network attitudes and skills exist along several dimensions: between older and younger researchers, between researchers and network administrators and managers, between people in different sectors, between researchers from different disciplines, and between researchers working on different kinds or different stages of problems. Because technology is constantly evolving, gaps in network skill among users will not disappear with the attrition of older researchers. Networks will always have to serve, and training will always have to meet the needs of, those in the 99th percentile of network skill, those in the 1st percentile, and everyone in between. Gaps in attitudes and skills must be reduced if network use is to become more universal and well-integrated into professional activities. Such gaps also cause organizational discord.

Key Issue 4: Access

Previous research has shown that degree of access to networks is associated with degree of use. The findings of this study suggest that the concept of access must be broadened to include other aspects as well, such as the potential user's:

- AWARENESS OF AVAILABLE INFORMATION AND TECHNOLOGY RESOURCES: Do researchers know of the network functions and capabilities available to them?

- ORGANIZATIONAL CULTURE: Does the organizational culture of the researcher permit and actively support networking?

- ATTITUDE TOWARD INFORMATION AND COMMUNICATION TECHNOLOGIES: Do researchers perceive information and communication technologies as a benefit or barrier to their investigations?

- AVAILABLE TECHNICAL EXPERTISE: Do researchers themselves have sufficient skill and training to use networks?

- FINANCIAL RESOURCES: Do researchers have sufficient resources to use networks when and how they want to?

On a national level, the results of this study indicate that network access, especially as defined above, is far from universal. Many institutions have:

- No physical connection to the network

- Inadequate hardware, software, and facilities

- Inadequate institutional support for and interest in the marketing of networks

- Limited user interest in and knowledge of networks

- Unequal support of disciplines (i.e., the physical and computational sciences receive the most support).

Many people fear that the Matthew effect (i.e., the rich get richer) will not only govern the distribution of network support of various kinds but also that the distinction between the information rich and the information poor will be exacerbated by the need for expensive technology and technical expertise. Researchers with network support will most likely obtain the greatest share of the resources and reputation needed to engage in scientific work.

Key Issue 5: Sector Differences and Relationships

As noted earlier, the proposed NREN is intended to serve researchers and other users in at least three major sectors: private corporations, academia, and Federal laboratories. In a very basic way, the three sectors have different goals and different standards by which the success or failure of an institution or researcher is measured. Academic institutions' primary reason for being, despite all the more "realistic" and economic reasons, is the advancement of knowledge. Federal laboratories exist in order to make discoveries which will advance human understanding and contribute to the military, economic, and social well-being of the nation. Private sector organizations exist primarily for profit.

Potential conflict among these users of a national research network may exist. In the private sector site, for example, there is subtle but real influence which discourages researchers from collaborating with researchers outside the corporation. Organizational culture often determines acceptance of innovation, so consideration of cultural factors must be included in the design and operation of a national network. In addition, disregard of sector differences will result in less national coordination and collaboration and more conflict among the different sectors.

Key Issue 6: Network Design and Management

Very few of the researchers who participated in this study had given any extended thought to future network policy development. They assumed that the status quo would always be maintained, i.e., that there would never be any restrictions placed on their network activities beyond voluntary compliance with general guidelines on acceptable use that had been developed by their own community.

Specifically, most researchers believed that:

- Self-regulation by researchers in accord with the norms of science should continue as the only form of network control.

- The government should support network development without imposing control.

- In principle, universal access should be guaranteed to "qualified users."

Researchers stated, in no uncertain terms, that any form of restriction on communication was abhorrent to science and detrimental to scientific productivity. At the same time, however, researchers apparently appreciate neither the constraints under which managers operate nor the difficulty of resolving conflicts among users, especially across sectors.

Key Issue 7: Difficulty of Measuring Productivity Increases and Other Benefits

Many of the researchers that took part in the study had the opinion that the benefits and importance of networks are so obvious that evaluation is not necessary or that only scientists' peers can judge the value of scientific work and networks' part in it.

This observation underscores some conceptual difficulties in evaluating the success of the NREN. These difficulties arise from the nature of information itself and of the scientific enterprise, e.g.:

- There is no validated, agreed upon method for determining the value of information in general, and information gained from networks specifically.

- We do not have the conceptual tools to measure the impact of a "good idea."

- It is virtually impossible to measure the benefit of broadening one's community, one of the major positive effects of electronic networks.

These conceptual difficulties indicate that the expectation of easily measurable productivity gains from the implementation of an NREN may be unrealistic. Study participants also insisted that the NREN should be considered as an investment in infrastructure. In addition, such an investment in the infrastructure may take ten or fifteen years or more to pay dividends.

Key Issue 8: Networks Magnify Existing Tendencies, Patterns, and Preferences

Electronic networks are not introduced into a social, personal, or organizational vacuum. The study's findings suggest that networks do not so much alter existing inclinations, attitudes, and behaviors as support, magnify, or extend them. For example, most researchers claim that networks facilitated, rather than changed the nature of, their work. It seems that many researchers try to incorporate networks into their existing communication and research styles and existing scientific norms.

Key Issue 9: Technophoria

"Technophoria" is a blind belief in the beneficial effects of technology and an identification of technology as the panacea for all kinds of problems. Just as with its counterpart, technophobia, the major difficulty with technophoria is its absolute character -- all technology is good, all problems have technical solutions, the only important problems are those that can be solved with technology, and technical experts should be the first and final arbiters of all conflicts.

Technophoria is especially pernicious because it can cause policy makers, the general public, and network users to develop unrealistic expectations about the power and benefits of networks. This leads to neglect of social and behavioral problems, of any problem beyond the technical and financial. The immense benefits of the NREN can be realized only by curbing technophoria and addressing the wider social issues.

Key Issue 10: Elitism

Currently, the "elite" control network development. High status researchers have access to more resources, including information technology resources, in most organizations. Researchers (1) with significant technical expertise, (2) at major research institutions, and (3) in certain highly supported natural and computational science disciplines are at a significant advantage socially as well as professionally when compared to other scientists or nonusers of networks.

One of the primary reasons for the establishment of an NREN is to ensure a "level playing field" for researchers so that all available expertise is brought to bear on research problems. Attention to technical and financial problems alone will not ensure full NREN participation by the vast majority of U.S. researchers.

Elitist practice leads to elitist versions of network management strategies, e.g., networks should be managed and used only by technical experts, and network policy should be decided by councils of prestigious scientists. Such high profile users often do not explicitly recognize their elite status. A fully integrated and accessible national network must overcome elitist attitudes in order to realize the greatest benefit from the national investment in an NREN.

Recommendations for the NREN

Our assessment of existing policy instruments, network literature, and our own empirical findings leads us to offer a number of recommendations to reduce the problems and barriers faced by users and help resolve the issues noted above.

Recommendation 1: Design the NREN in Light of User Information Needs and Behavior

While it is clear that networks must meet a broad range of goals, they cannot meet those goals unless they are designed to accommodate user information needs. In recent publications regarding network development and information policy alternatives, the role and importance of the user seem to have been set aside. As the nation continues the design of the NREN, decision makers and policy makers must make certain that spokespersons for users and the manner in which users actually gather and use information contribute to the design of such services and policies.

Recommendation 2: Require Direct Support for Network Training

Policy should be developed that requires the NREN to allocate a certain percentage of its resources for training and education purposes. Thus, if the NREN is budgeted at $400 million, the law might indicate that 8%(or some percentage) of that total budget must be dedicated to education and training. The disposition of these funds could also help to assure a "level playing field," maximize national investment in R&D, and limit network elitism.

A number of interviewees commented that if the Federal government did not require resources to be spent on training, institutions would not engage in meaningful programs of user education. Indeed, the key here is the need for programs of education and training. Having one or two individuals who will respond to demand does not constitute an educational program.

Recommendation 3: Obtain Greater Involvement From the Library Community

The role of libraries in the development and implementation of NREN is just beginning to be explored. Reports by some of the key players in the Federal government have given little attention to how the library community could be involved. This situation is somewhat paradoxical given that community's experiences with bibliographic utilities such as OCLC, online databases, and other national networking applications.

More specifically, the involvement of the library community could take a number of directions, such as:

- Affirmation of the role of the library community as a major stakeholder in the development of any national networking initiative

- Provision of network access to selected bibliographic utilities

- Provision of personalized electronic reference services to researchers

- Development of directories and indexes (print and online) to network services

- Promotion of and training for network use.

These are only a few of the possibilities. Library leaders knowledgeable about the NREN and electronic networks should be actively and immediately involved in a range of planning activities.

Recommendation 4: Provide Better Documentation and Directories

Significant improvements in the use and impact of the NREN can result from improving documentation for the range of network uses and applications available. Such documentation should be written from a problem–solving perspective rather than with a technical orientation. In addition, directories of the broad range of available information resources and services, access techniques, and individuals involved in networking are also needed to increase the usefulness of networks.

Many users are less interested in "why" something works than in "how" to make it work. Technically intensive and detailed documentation, print or online, is often counterproductive. Also, existing knowledge about graphic presentations, integrating text with graphics, and producing high-impact publications or online information, paradoxically, frequently fails to find its way into the production of network documentation.

Recommendation 5: Develop Mechanisms to Improve Communication Between Network Engineers/Managers and Network Users

The evidence from the study suggests that there are two very different perspectives on how networks should be used, how they should be designed, and how they might be managed. Generally, network engineers and managers have a technical, hardware perspective while users tend to be oriented more to applications and problem–solving. Unfortunately, there is oftentimes little effective communication between these two groups.

Findings from the study suggest that network engineers, managers, and support personnel are perceived by the users as "out of touch" with users' computing needs and fixated on technology. Users are often perceived by the engineers and managers as unwilling or unable to learn and use the new technologies. Users are seen as naive about the constraints under which networks are designed and managed, while users say that network engineers and managers do not understand the process of integrating technology into research and scientific communication.

The successful development of electronic networks in support of research and scientific communication will require regular and effective communication between network users and network engineers and managers.

Recommendation 6: Conduct Additional Research

The current basis for decision making regarding the NREN is inadequate. Some important research questions to be answered are:

* Is there a competitive advantage for scientists who use electronic networks?

* Do electronic networks exacerbate inequalities between the information "haves" and "have-nots"?

* What user–based factors should be taken into consideration in the design and operation of networks?

* Who will bring network resources under "bibliographic" control (i.e., organizing, describing, and providing access points) to make them available to all kinds of users?

* What types of educational programs, delivery techniques, and topics are most important for specific types of users?

* How are scientists' attitudes toward scientific norms related to their actual network behavior?

As suggested earlier, there is much more speculation and "opinionating" about the use, design, impact, benefits, and roles of an NREN than there is empirically based evidence. If policy makers determine that an NREN should be supported, they should also support (1) research to aid in the design of the network, and (2) ongoing evaluation and research into the network's performance.

Realizing the Promise of the NREN

The claims that electronic networks will lead to significant increases in productivity, enhanced national competitiveness, and making "everyone" a better scientist or researcher must be tempered by awareness of the range of social and behavioral issues that need to be addressed and resolved. Indeed, the technical problems and issues associated with the design and operation of the NREN are likely to be easier to resolve than the social and behavioral issues identified in this study. It is especially important that the library community, with its skills and knowledge of users and meeting user information needs, becomes actively involved in the decision making for the design and operation of the NREN.

Dr. Charles R. McClure is a professor and Ann Bishop, Philip Doty, and Howard Rosenbaum are doctoral students at the School of Information Studies, Syracuse University, Syracuse, NY 13244.

The Future of the National Research and Education Network

Dr. John R. Garrett

Copyright Clearance Center

In the next few minutes I will talk about basic principles which, in my view, must provide the foundation for the ideas behind the NREN. Discussion of basic principles, in our society, tend to begin with either the Bible or the Constitution.

Unfortunately, however, despite much effort I have been unable to find any support for the assertion of many publishers that there was a c with a circle around it carved into the tree of life. Nor could I find any evidence for the view of some in the library community that the snake in the Garden of Eden really worked for Elsevier. So the Constitution will have to do.

Article One, Section Eight, establishes the fundamental powers of the Congress. Among those powers is the power "to promote the progress of science and useful arts, by securing for a limited time, to authors and inventors, the exclusive right, to their respective writings and discoveries." Expanding on this section in Federalist Paper #43, James Madison, the principal author of the Constitution, added: "The utility of this power will scarcely be questioned. The copy right of authors has been solemnly adjudged in Great Britain to be a right at common law. The right to useful inventions, seems with equal reason to belong to the inventors. The public good fully coincides in both cases, with the claims of individuals."

What does this mean now? If, as Madison argued, "The public good fully coincides with the claims of individuals," then it is impossible to separate the property right of creators of intellectual property which is imbedded in the Constitution, from the society's right to information.

How does all of this relate to the National Research and Education Network? The vision of the NREN embodies information available to everyone at a price which sustains, extends and supports creators and ensures widespread access. Questions are currently being raised about whether this system

-- which incorporates both the right of creators to their property and the right of society to information -- can really work in an electronic age.

Three main issues are currently being raised by those who argue that it cannot. First, some believe, a comprehensive electronic system such as that contemplated in the NREN would embody too many transactions and would be too complex to actually manage and support ownership of intellectual property. In my view, this position ignores the fact that counting things is what computers do best -- in fact, it is all they know how to do. Second, this argument assumes some kind of transactional system which actually counts and charges for individual transactions. The Copyright Clearance Center (CCC) believes that broad-based licenses are a more interesting approach to these problems, and we are currently exploring a variety of licensing options.

The second objection raised is that it is impossible to identify who owns what in an electronic age. The computer, it is argued, permits modification and revision easily and seamlessly, without leaving behind any clear record of when and where the materials were modified. This is a real issue. Various parties are exploring a variety of technical fixes which could resolve it, but it is not resolved yet. One technical fix is suggested in a recent report by the Corporation for National Research Initiatives (CNRI) on intellectual property in the electronic age. This question will need to be addressed more seriously than it has been to date.

A third argument against retaining our current intellectual property system in the electronic age is personified by "those nasty publishers." This argument, presented sometimes by librarians, at other times by authors or information entrepreneurs, includes: "They make too much money," "They are too slow," "They have too much power," and "They already publish too many things anyway." Publishers have answered these arguments in many other forums, and do not need my responses added to theirs. I would remind users, including librarians, however, that the "Too much money," "Too much power," and "Too many publications" are a direct result of creators creating intellectual property and users using it. It is difficult to sustain an argument which proposes moving toward a freer market on the one hand, while criticizing publishers for having operated in a free market in the past on the other.

There are a series of other basic questions which arise from the National Research and Education Network which will need to be addressed as we all begin to move forward into this transformed age. First, what does "own" mean in an electronic age? That question is easy to answer in a paper world, because it is simple to differentiate between altered copies and originals. In an electronic age, it will be difficult or impossible to determine the difference between an "original" and "a modified copy." That determination may not even be useful. But if we are to retain traditional views of ownership, we will need to rethink what owning means.

Second, we need to look carefully at who should develop the National Research and Education Network. There are powerful reasons for involving government -- at least the Federal Government -- in this process. Most powerful, of course, is access to federal funds. Some have argued that the Federal Government should be used to support the development of the NREN, and then move out on implementation. This seems to me to present a naive view of the relationship between funding and control. There are serious issues to be addressed should government (federal, state or local) have a substantial role in managing or controlling the NREN. These concerns include privacy, open access to information, and the relationship between domestic or international government policy and the information requirements of an increasingly knowledge-thirsty public.

Third, no one in my view has thought through carefully enough who is going to pay for the NREN and how prices will be established. In the print world, publishers have learned over the years to estimate the value of their information. This value is built out of a complicated set of calculations involving, among other factors, cost and an estimate of the size and value of the potential market. All of these calculations need to be rethought in an electronic information world. There is, of course, some experience in

these directions through Dialog, Bibliographic Retrieval Service, and other information providers, but it is not comprehensive or broad-based enough to respond to all of the needs of a fully articulated electronic system.

Then who pays? If users pay, the cost of system infrastructure, as well as of information, may lead to charges which will seem more than the market will bear. If user-paid costs do not include infrastructure, etc., then we are back at substantial government support with the risks and concerns that I have raised earlier. There are no simple answers to these questions; indeed, any answers will grow out of an ongoing, messy dialog among the various participants, rather than out of any conceptual formulation in forums such as this.

Finally, when and how will it all happen? Long ingrained habits, such as the habitual ways in which we use information, change slowly. It is interesting to note that this discussion of transformation of the way we use written material occurs in a forum which is essentially unchanged since the fourteenth century. Indeed, a professor from the University of Paris of that time, walking into the back of this room, would find the setting very familiar. One bunch of people sits and listens to another smaller group which is at a raised level. This scenario has not changed in seven hundred years. He might be confused by the slides, but as the slides are read by the speaker, he would not be confused for long.

For the transformation of learning that we contemplate through the NREN to accelerate, we need to better understand the social context in which new learning occurs. We need, in particular, to look at the few examples we have of generalized, universal, worldwide learning systems. The only two world learning systems today are, of course, Nintendo and Rock and Roll. If we understood better why fifteen year old children know the lyrics to the same songs in the United States that they bop to in the Philippines, we might have a better idea how to generate the world-wide access and use which is promised by the NREN. This is the level of questions we need to address, and which will raise many other questions to follow.

Dr. John R. Garrett is director of market development, Copyright Clearance Center, 27 Congress St., Salem, MA 01970.

Libraries in the 21st Century

What We Should Do With NREN

Susan K. Martin

Georgetown University

There is an immediate need for the library profession to think critically about libraries, librarians, technology, and the future. These subjects are broader than NREN, and they *include* NREN. We as a profession must look seriously at ourselves, at the institutions we consider our competition, and at our future. We must identify the role that we really want to play in an information society, and set to work sculpting that role.

The issue here is one of encouraging a large and diverse profession to view itself differently from the way it does today. We need to ensure that the services that we offer *now* will continue to be supported and offered in the future, while we simultaneously support the information services required because increasing amounts of information are available electronically. No matter what we tell ourselves, we may not be offering the right services to attract and hold the attention of all levels of society. It is well and good to represent motherhood and apple pie, and to satisfy the needs of small children, scholars, and senior citizens. However, that is not the entirety of the role that will create for libraries an important and appropriate niche in the information society.

We used to be in the lead, as far as information technology is concerned. Back in the 1960s, when we were automating cataloging, acquisitions, and circulation, information technology was a new thing, not at all pervasive throughout society. When librarians came along and did what the computer types finally couldn't do -- automate variable-length and complex records -- the profession was recognized as being in the forefront of the technological revolution. We recognized it ourselves, but began at that time to wonder how we would manage to stay in the lead.

Actually, that lead has not dissipated as much as some of us tend to think. I would suggest that after the telecommunications people, the computer and networks people, we may well be next in line with a gradually building interest in and concern for the concept of NREN and the services that we can provide.

What Should Libraries Be in the Next Century?

To answer that question, many of us have tried to determine what the future library should be like. We have been exposed to the paperless society; the library without walls; the move from collections to access; the shift in emphasis from quantity to quality. You have read many articles and even books about the need to move our institutions in any of these directions. For the past fifteen or twenty years our literature has been replete with scenarios which describe one or more of these phenomena.

Very little has happened as a result of these efforts to conceptualize a library of the future. Libraries have certainly changed but they have evolved in rather predictable ways, chiefly as a result of automating the bibliographic record. The four concepts I just mentioned -- paperless society, library without walls, collections to access, and quantity to quality -- remain primarily that: concepts. We can't seem to put these ideas to work for us. We have a problem peculiar to an institution which must look backward at the same time that it is moving forward. As we do this, we are likely to stumble, because we are not looking at where we are going.

At least for the moment, it is imperative that we continue to support traditional library functions; after all, most information is still produced on paper, and read on paper. This need to remain preoccupied with the traditional library has caused us to talk *about* the library of the future, without really *doing* too much about it. If we don't reconceptualize our own institutions, can we expect the rest of the world to do it for us? No, but the rest of the world will invent the information services it needs and place them in institutions other than libraries, because we have not stepped up to take responsibility for serving society in the information age or even reminded them that we are here. This usurpation of a role we should be playing is already taking place, with a phenomenon barely twenty years old: the for-profit information delivery services sector is thriving.

We need to refocus and redefine *part* of our services. There is no question that the traditional library is *not only* motherhood and apple pie, it is essential and libraries must offer basic services without charge. We do things that no one else would do, because we have defined as a part of our mission those elements of information service that would never be profitable in a business environment, that serve anyone, whether they pay or not. That is good, and we should continue to serve this role. However, we must not cast aside the role of information provider to the "haves", using the most advanced information technologies, and yes, charging for services, particularly where they are customized to answer just one patron's information need.

Most of our parent institutions fund us only to carry out the traditional library's role. The new, the innovative, have been regarded as rather a luxury, to be funded by grants or other soft money, but certainly never to come out of the operating budget. Some very small number of our colleagues has been successful in persuading their parent institutions that innovative information technologies are a necessary addition to, and not a replacement for, the traditional library and require added funding.

Since we haven't yet created our own vision of the future of libraries, it is a corollary that we haven't been able to convey a new and different vision to our governing bodies. We absolutely must do this, and we are at a point in history where we must seize the opportunity or lose the business.

Semantics are at issue, and I am as guilty as anyone else. We continue to talk about innovative information technologies and the library of the future, as though these were phenomena that are not imminent and not understandable. One step we need to take is to stop talking in these terms, and instead talk about how to deliver access to *existing electronic information* to our patrons, who are the same patrons as before and who continue to require access to *all* recorded knowledge in all formats, to the extent that any single library can provide it directly or remotely.

Are We Going to be Two Professions?

In the early part of this century, splinter groups of librarians became dissatisfied with the large, unwieldy, and conservative American Library Association. They split off to create other groups, among them the Special Libraries Association and the American Society for Information Science. Are we gradually heading down a path that will lead to another break-point in the way our profession perccives itself? I suggest that evidence points clearly in that direction, and that such an occurrence might not be at all bad.

I can envision a group of librarians, frustrated by the lack of the main body of the profession to cope with obvious issues such as the ones I have been talking about, remaining members of ALA but simultaneously organizing another group. Let us call it the Association of Information Providers. Represented in this group would be the people who are willing to adopt change, including the change in the nature of the library. That is, fee or free would not be in question; it would be understood by this group that information costs money, and however a university, company or municipality wishes to bear these costs, the information seeking public eventually pays, either directly for customized information or indirectly through taxes, tuition, or other means.

The Association of Information Providers is not limited to librarians. Among its membership are publishers who recognize that their institution also requires them to operate differently than they have in the past, and also information brokers. More than ever, we are seeing a call for a revision of copyright, which is a vehicle designed to protect intellectual property in an age that no longer exists. Some publishers are beginning to discern that their role will change, and they are no longer fighting the copyright wars. To let you know how serious they are, the Association of American Publishers is fully engaged in the process of helping to organize NET '91, the meeting sponsored by EDUCOM, Association of Research Libraries (ARL), and others, to address issues raised by NREN and other pieces of a nationwide network.

Remaining outside this organization would be the folks who say that the library should be traditional and free. Their libraries will become the welfare information institutions; they will serve anyone and everyone with whatever resources they can manage to pull together. Certainly electronic information, which costs money at a different level and in a different way than does print on paper, will not be offered by these libraries. Gradually the information seeking public who are willing and have the capacity to pay for information will go elsewhere, because elsewhere they can find not only the traditional sources but also the world of electronic information, including access to Internet or NREN.

We still have an opportunity to become a force. Although a relatively small segment of society is involved with NREN thus far, those who are involved are powerful and have not until recently seen libraries as relevant to the discussion of NREN. We have begun to change their perceptions; earlier this year a group of people representing several library associations, Chief Officers of State Library Agencies (COSLA) and National Commission on Libraries and Information Science (NCLIS) met together to agree upon language that could be suggested to Congress as changes to the NREN legislation. Many of the suggestions were incorporated in the more recent drafting of the bill, and the librarians are responsible for major changes such as: dropping the word "higher" so that NREN now refers to all levels of education; incorporating the national libraries as obvious participants in the NREN process; and including a bibliographic function to make it possible to locate information that might be accessible through the NREN.

The role of the librarians in this discussion is critical. The traditional computer user is not a traditional information seeker, and the traditional computer center administrator is not a traditional provider of information services. Librarians possess the skill of providing information with a concern for service, and should bring these traits to the development of the nationwide network, in the interest of the information–seeking and –using public.

Librarians belong in a knowledge culture, and need to be among the leaders. This new arena is one in which we will have to face up to issues of copyright, payment, and other nasty things that we have avoided scrupulously in the past. I am convinced that to remain alive and vital, we will not be able to avoid them in the future, nor can we come to the table to deal with our colleagues with such belligerence that no one wants to work with the library community.

Libraries are a reflection of our society; if it changes, we also change. Since we are the ones who presume to know how to handle and locate information, we should be leading in this redefinition.

As a part of this process, librarians will have to admit that information is not free, and depending on the way it is delivered, may have to be charged for. This is uncomfortable to many, but the alternative is to become the museum, the welfare information kiosk. We do not want to permit these alternatives to foster a role in society that would relegate us to the back burner.

To turn our libraries into information centers of the future will require that we stimulate change within our own institutions. Even more, we need to rethink the library, and convey that reconceptualization to the rest of the world. We need to show them that libraries (or information centers) are exciting, nontraditional, places where computer technology allows access to more information for more people than ever before. Let me quote from Paul Gherman's testimony on behalf of ARL in support of the High–Performance Computer Technology Act of 1990: "The vision I have just drawn for you is one filled with great promise, where information will be efficiently produced, accessed, and delivered almost instantaneously directly to the scholar, researcher, and scientist. It is a future of information riches which could transform the scholarly communication process, making our researchers more efficient and productive in their work. But beyond the technical issues there are many other difficult legal, standards, and management issues. Before we can realize this future, a significant rethinking of intellectual property rights and copyright law must be undertaken. The original vision for the NREN was to make supercomputing more broadly available to scientists and researchers. It was a very worthwhile initiative. However, I believe the vision the library community has presented to you here today sees in the NREN the possibility of transforming the very basis of scholarly communication in our nation." I would add only two sentences: My vision of the NREN would have it gradually transforming the basis of communication of information at *all* levels, to *all* people who need information, throughout the nation. Let us cease our arguments over fee versus free, stop verbally designing the library of the future, and get to work on realizing the *promise* of the future.

Susan K. Martin is university librarian, Georgetown University, Washington, D.C., and was formerly executive director of NCLIS.

Visions of a National Network

Data Networks and the Academic Library

CRAIG A. SUMMERHILL

Washington State University

Background

In November 1987, the National Science Foundation provided funding to be managed by the Merit Computer Network (Michigan) over a five year period, in cooperation IBM and MCI, to re-engineer and expand the backbone of the National Science Foundation Network (NSFNET). Since July 1988, data traffic on the network has increased approximately twenty percent per month.[1] Such profound growth illustrates the fact that higher education in the United States is entering a new age of mass communication and data transfer, and nowhere on American campuses are the shock waves being felt more fully than in the library.

Currently, there are over 100,000 computers linked to the NSFNET. Within ten years, there will be 500,000. The number of active users on the network is projected to increase from the current one million to four-to-six million users by the turn of the century. Such growth offers clear justification for the proposed National Research and Education Network (NREN) — a "data superhighway" to be built largely around the NSFNET infrastructure.

Connecting Campus Networks

Nearly all colleges and universities in the United States provide some level of access to the many converging data networks such as BITNET, CSNET, Internet, and the NSFNET. The network user in the academic world is a faculty member, an administrator, a member of the support staff, or most importantly — a student. National networking is challenging professors to realize that the classroom experience is no longer confined to the space and time between the classroom walls.

[1]. International Business Machines. *NSFNET – The National Science Foundation Computer Network for Research and Education* (Milford, CT: IBM, Academic Information Systems, 1990), p. 14–15.

Similarly, the age of the academic "library without walls" is dawning, not of its own volition, but driven largely by forces external to libraries. Electronic communication with other students, professors, researchers, and even businessmen is having a profound impact on traditional methods of information gathering and dissemination in the academic community. Information which formerly took months to publish in traditional print formats can currently be distributed to a growing worldwide audience in a few short hours. For example, following the recent and much celebrated announcement of a successful cold-fusion experiment at the University of Utah, interested physicists were sharing vital data related to the experiment via a distributed mailing list within days of the announcement.

The essence of the interpersonal communication process is being shaken at its foundation as a result of electronic communication. The electronic transmission of text allows many people to converse at their leisure. Unlike a telephone call, textual messages sent on Monday can be answered on Tuesday with no disruption in the flow of the conversation. Because this process does not require the shared temporal periods necessary for speech (i.e. telephone calls), this process is termed "non real-time communication." Ironically, the hallmark of libraries, namely the book, had a similar effect upon societal communication in the Western world following the advent of moveable type.

Network Services

Electronic distribution of text is simply one method in which data can be disseminated via the network. Any information stored in binary can be transferred as a digital signal over the network. Voice, music, still image graphics, and full motion video, can all be transmitted, provided sufficient data capacity (termed bandwidth) exists to move the signal. Given digital technology, a professor at MIT could store a lecture which includes videotape footage, color images (formerly slides or transparencies), and the text of a homework assignment. Transmitted across the network, the lecture could be viewed concurrently at UC Berkeley, or recorded in California and retransmitted at a later date.

Other benefits the academic community derives from national networking include the cost–sharing of expensive scientific instruments and immediate access to widely dispersed databases. Geographically isolated researchers can share equipment by either transmitting data to the equipment for processing, or logging onto another computer across the network. This prevents two institutions from making similar investments to operate the same equipment. Thus astronomers at MIT and at UC Berkeley can each analyze data from the Hubble Space Telescope across the network by pooling their resources. Any data generated as a result of research and experimentation is increasingly being stored for statistical processing by computers. The provision of an open systems computing model guarantees that all users can utilize this data regardless of their physical location on the network.

Future Trends: The Academic Library Challenge

The provision of information services on the network, chiefly through access to widely dispersed databases, poses the greatest challenge to the academic library community. Organizing and classifying large bodies of electronic data into information formats valuable to the user demands resources that exceed those available to most academic libraries. To date, the focal point of automated library systems has been to provide bibliographic information, but academic users are increasingly demanding full text and multi–media information resources which exceed the data processing capabilities of these systems. The provision of personalized information services in a non real–time environment is also challenging the basis of traditional library services.

Today, America is clearly the world leader in networking technology. To keep this edge in the next decade, and the coming century, the library must move beyond the confining walls of the building. Academic librarians must provide both vocal support for national networks such as the NREN, and educated leadership in the development of data networks which provide information services to all segments of society, all types of organizations, and all different genres of libraries.

Craig A. Summerhill is assistant systems librarian at Washington State University, and is currently chair of the Library and Information Technology Association's Telecommunications Interest Group.

A Public Library Perspective on the NREN

LOIS M. KERSHNER

Peninsula Libraries Automated Network

The last paragraph of the *Resolution on a National Research and Education Network* submitted by the LITA Board of Directors (and endorsed by the LAMA Board of Directors) to the ALA Legislation Committee at the Chicago 1990 Midwinter Meeting states:

> RESOLVED   That the American Library Association work to improve legislative and other proposals to increase opportunities for **multitype** library participation in and contributions to the National Research and Education Network.

This clear statement recognizes a potential role for public libraries as well as those of the academic and corporate community in the development and opportunity of a National Research and Education Network (NREN).

A brief review of articles addressing the NREN indicates that present network access best serves persons associated with institutions of higher education or large corporations with industrial laboratories where the technological development and funding have been made available. Access to existing networks, each with its databases and/or supercomputing and conferencing capabilities, is through institutional affiliation. For example, from a single workstation a staff member could not only access the institution's library online catalog and other databases mounted locally, but also switch through inter-network bridges to databases at other institutions, other data services, and bibliographic utilities.

The articulation of the larger vision for the National Research and Education Network broadens the view beyond institutional affiliation, to a "workplace without walls." As Erich Bloch has stated:

> [The national network] is a facility in which a full range of the nation's intellectual resources--databases, libraries, computers, and people--are universally accessible to researchers and educators. In this new context, 'remote' no longer means 'isolated', and the concept of 'scholar' is

restored to its historic significance denoting a practitioner of a portable profession.[1]

Provision of information access for researchers and scholars is not limited to research and corporate libraries, however. The public research library has defined as its role the assistance to scholars and researchers as they conduct in-depth studies, investigate specific areas of knowledge, and create new knowledge. The needs of the individual may well go beyond the collection strengths of the public research library, speaking to the need for access to the resources available through a National Research and Education Network.

The independent scholar whose library of residence is not a public research library has information access needs no different from those of colleagues living in close proximity to one. Indeed, any individual not associated with an institution already on a network can benefit from access to information resources on the NREN. Any public library therefore has the potential need, on behalf of its patrons, for connection to the NREN, whether by direct linkage to the network or indirectly through relationships with other regional institutions.

Unlike academic and corporate research libraries, however, with access to such a network through institutional affiliation, the public library itself bears the full expense of network linkage. While public and other libraries can apply for grants to help bear the cost of linking to a network, for example from the National Science Foundation to link to the NSFNET, public funding must be made available to ensure that access to information can be both available and affordable.

Now is the time that technological, access, funding, and governance issues for the National

---

[1]. Erich Bloch. "A National Network: Today's Reality, Tomorrow's Vision, Part 1," *EDUCOM Bulletin* 23,2/3 (Summer/Fall 1988), p. 11.

Research and Education Network are being addressed. Now is the time for the public library to be an active advocate for its needs, to ensure they are built into planning during the formative years of NREN, so that the broader vision of access to information in the "workplace without walls" becomes a reality.

Lois Kershner is project director for the Peninsula Libraries Automated Network, 25 Tower Road, Belmont, California 94002, and is a past president of LITA.

Electronic Networking for California State and Public Libraries

GARY STRONG, KATHY HUDSON AND JOHN JEWELL

California State Library

State libraries and public libraries in the United States have valuable contributions to offer the users of a network such as the proposed National Research and Education Network (NREN). Our California State Library serves as a public research library, provides for the information and library needs of state government, and works for the development and promotion of public library services for all Californians. The MELVYL™ system, in fact, includes the California State Library in addition to the nine University of California libraries. It is a source of pride to me as State Librarian, and to our staff, that we are a net lender, not a net borrower, with these major research libraries.

Throughout its 140 year history, the California State Library has acquired important works. Far West explorer John C. Freemont was one of the first contributors. The Sutro family of San Francisco fame provided the nucleus for an extensive local history and genealogy collection. The Paul Gann Archive contains the personal records of the originator of a tax revolt that rocked the nation's public sector. Nearly 3,000,000 records from newspapers, periodicals and books about California persons, places, and events are included in the California Room information files. The Government Publications Section is the only complete federal depository library in California and produces printed indexes to state publications.

The State Library recognizes the importance of electronic access for its own holdings, with over 500,000 RLIN records already in the MELVYL™ system. Plans are close to completion to add over 200,000 federal document records, and a major retrospective conversion project is well underway for older state documents. Like the Oregon State Library, which has brought up a variety of public information databases, we know that to serve our clientele we must provide more than our own bibliographic holdings. The State Library's own integrated library system, presently being installed, supports NISO standards and can mount non–MARC databases. It can link to a variety of external information sources, including, in a test, TCP/IP links to MELVYL™ and the Internet. The State Library's planning, still in draft, includes providing electronic access for state agencies and public libraries to our holdings and to these other resources.

Public and special libraries in the state have their own unique contributions. For example, the extensive holdings of the Los Angeles, San Francisco, and San Diego public libraries have long been recognized as key research sources. Fresno County Free Library has one of the world's finest collections on William Saroyan. The California Institute of the Arts Library has more than 16,000 music scores, approximately 10,000 art exhibition catalogs, a large collection of screenplays, and the Los Angeles Institute of Contemporary Artists' Registry with data and slides on contemporary southern California artists.

The State Library has an active, positive role in helping libraries make such resources accessible. The California Statewide Data Base on OCLC is an ongoing project to build and maintain an automated database of the current acquisitions of California public libraries. It contains nearly 9,000,000 California public library holdings records. Significant special reference resources from 93 public and special libraries were made available through last year's Telefacsimile Networking Grants (LSCA), including those of the California Institute of the Arts Library.

As Edwin Brownrigg points out in *Developing the Information Superhighway: Issues for Libraries*, implementation of NREN requires more than solving technical communication problems. It involves complex policy, procedural, governance and financing issues. A battery of California library programs are helping lay a foundation. Libraries in the state are carefully building the structure for a multi-type network. A new model for reference referral, also recognizing contributions of all types of libraries, is under development and will provide access to high quality reference for all Californians. The state-funded (CLSA) Transaction Based Reimbursements Program provides a strong basis to encourage libraries to provide materials to other than their own clientele, assisting with direct loans of over 16,000,000 and interlibrary loans of over 460,000.

The State Library and California public libraries have a valuable role in linking our users to the proposed NREN resources. Access to NREN by our libraries is critical to our mission to provide accurate, timely, and responsive reference and information service to our patrons. Moreover, our ability to provide access to specialized databases and current research relevant to public policy is of critical importance to ongoing support of NREN, whether it be current status of earthquake prediction or superconductor research. The majority of policy planners and decision-makers in the state will form their impressions of libraries based upon the quality and level of information they receive through the State Library and public library service programs.

In California, as in the rest of the nation, entrepreneurial spirit is viewed as critical in state industries for maintaining a competitive edge in the world market. Most of the companies in our high technology centers have or began with fifty or fewer employees. For these companies, there is no major research facility or corporate library. The local public libraries provide strong support as research resources for such companies. The California State Library has encouraged and supported such development, for example, through grants to projects like the Silicon Valley Information Center in the San Jose Public Library.

California's ethnically and racially diverse population poses a challenge to all public service organizations, and certainly to libraries--public, school, special and academic. The State Library has allocated over $4,000,000 in LSCA funds to assist community library service staff serving American Indian, Asian, Pacific, Black and Hispanic populations. We recently arranged with OCLC for the loading of Spanish language subject headings tapes. Asian Shared Information & Access (ASIA) continues to provide

machine- readable cataloged titles (over 130,000 copies) in Chinese, Japanese, Korean, and Vietnamese languages to libraries serving readers of Asian languages.

In addition, the State Library and California public libraries have become increasingly concerned with the growing division between the information-rich and information-poor, with serious gaps created by social, economic, and geographic barriers. It is not enough to provide for delivery systems. Californians, to be full participants in the new networking and new economy, will require appropriate education. Although the rate of adult illiteracy in basic reading skills is staggering, the rate of information illiteracy in accessing and using more sophisticated information far exceeds this basic challenge. Public libraries have a responsibility to assist our patrons in developing information literacy. If we are to bridge this growing gap between the information-poor and the information-rich, we suggest an approach which does not require making every Californian information technology literate. It is mediated access through libraries that is realistic and appropriate. The libraries and their clientele can accept the value of the new technologies. The problem lies in equality of access. The public libraries serve as a base for such universal access for all Californians.

Free and equal access are hallmarks for the California State Library and, we believe, for the public librarians of California. Recently, a headline read "All Librarians Are Radicals". The author, Stewart Brand, commented:

> The only communicators taking full advantage of the electronic convergence of all media are the librarians, who owe allegiance to no single industry. In America librarians are officially sanctioned outlaws. They truly believe information ought to be free and follow wherever it explores ... libraries are major crafters of the emerging information infrastructure--infostructure [1].

[1] Stewart Brand. "Outlaws, Musicians, Lovers, and Spies: The Future of Control." *Whole Earth Review* 67 (Summer 1990), p. 130–135.

Gary Strong is California state librarian. Kathy Hudson, information technology coordinator, and John Jewell, library microsystems specialist, are also with the California State Library, Sacramento, CA.

The National Research and Education Network For Special Libraries

STEVE CISLER

Apple Computer Library

This brief paper discusses how the technical library at Apple Computer, Inc., is using the existing web of electronic networks and how an expanded broadband network might be used by this and other special libraries.

The Apple Library's mission is to help Apple employees obtain the information they need in a timely manner. Because the company's prime goal is to develop and sell innovative computers and related products, the library and its users place a premium on the speed of delivery of the information and its relevance to the researcher. That means we will use any means we can to communicate with the employee and to find the information. This includes face–to–face reference interviews, fax, phone, and extensive use of electronic mail. Much of our internal business is conducted on a variety of LAN–based electronic mail systems, all of which are connected to Apple-Link, an electronic mail, databank, and bulletin board system for use by employees, dealers, customers, and consultants around the world. To obtain the information, we rely on book jobbers, information brokers, and of course, commercial services such as Dialog, Dow Jones, and Mead Data Central. We access the latter via value–added packet switching networks.

Many engineers within Apple also use the Internet, the network of networks that will serve as the basis for the proposed National Research and Education Network. Apple's Engineering Computer Operations is a commercial member of BARRNet, a regional network that is part of the Internet. We have wide bandwidth networks within the company; the existing Internet is using a backbone network where the speed will be increasing from 1.56 megabits per second to 45 megabits per second in 1990. That is 18,750 times as fast as a 2400 baud connection. Researchers at distant Apple sites and in universities and government organizations keep in touch with their colleagues in Cupertino, California, and are able to quickly transfer large files between any part of the U.S. and Cupertino. There are mail links between AppleLink and the Internet, so that Apple engineers can send requests to the library any way they wish. Until recently, only two librarians have had Internet accounts, but with the increased awareness of library resources and discussion groups available through the Internet (and from BITNET), more than half the staff now uses *apple.com*, the computer that connects to the Internet. As more people begin to use electronic mail the Internet accounts are proving to have better connectivity than any other. At present we can exchange mail with researchers, librarians, and educators on BITNET, CompuServe, The WELL, Fidonet, FredNet, ALANET, UUCP––the Unix network, and various networks in Asia and Europe. There is no direct charge for connect time or packets of data transmitted, as there would be on Dialog or ALANET.

Most special libraries may not believe they need this sort of connectivity with so many other librarians or institutions. Admittedly, the addressing schemes are complex, and the list of bibliographic and database resources on the Internet is just being compiled. Finding useful information is for pioneers and explorers and may frustrate librarians used to having reliable printed directories or running a macro that immediately connects to Dialog and runs a search on Medline or Computer Database.

When the NREN becomes a reality, either through legislation or some other governmental involvement, the Internet will grow and change. The changes will result from an increase in bandwidth, an increase in member organizations (and membership may not even be the correct term if NREN becomes more of a commercial than a cooperative, government funded enterprise), and a diversity in services and users that is not present on the Internet in mid–1990. At present, the types of special libraries using this network are limited to some governmental organizations and libraries in computer manufacturing and software development firms as well as telecommunications companies. Various commercial vendors of network connectivity are appearing on the scene, including Performance Systems International, Inc., formed with part of the technical staff from NYSERNET in New York state, which is selling accounts to various commercial firms. Undoubtedly, some of those special libraries will come on line as the benefits become more apparent.

I predict that more special libraries will find NREN to be worth supporting, *after* it is established and new services are offered for a fee. At present The Research Libraries Group, the Colorado Alliance for Research Libraries, and Clarinet Software are about the only ones selling information to Internet users. All of it is currently textual information, but high data rates will make possible the transmission of images of journal articles, patents, sound and video clips, and large files from satellite data collection archives and engineering design and medical image databases.

Because the legislation emphasizes the eventual commercialization of the NREN, I am sure there will be many old and new firms that will do business online with special, academic, school, and public libraries. Another benefit of this network, if it is eventually used by many libraries, will be the ability of distant libraries to collaborate on projects, of professional associations to preplan annual conferences in ways that fax and phone do not allow. Video conferencing may be used to some extent but won't replace the face-to-face meetings. What will happen is that participants will exchange a great deal more information prior to meeting, and virtual communities of members who live far from each other will grow stronger.

The opinions expressed in this short essay are those of the author; Apple Computer, Inc. may not agree with all of them. Comments or questions may be sent to Steve Cisler, Apple Computer Library, 10381 Bandley Drive, MS: 8C, Cupertino, California 95014. (408) 974–3258. Internet address: sac@apple.com.

Electronic Networking at Davis Senior High School

Janet Meizel

Davis Senior High School, Davis, California

In the immediate future, much of our research and communication will be handled by computer-based telecommunications. This has created new opportunities for the business world and new problems for those in the field of education who must provide students with the appropriate skills to use in that world. The necessary skills should be taught to high school students before they enter the job market, but programs to accomplish this task are expensive and equipment available to students is often out of date.

A unique partnership was formed in the K–12 educational arena to try to resolve this problem. Under the auspices of a grant from Pacific Bell and assistance from the Internet Federation, Davis (Calif.) Senior High School (DSHS) and the University of California, Davis (UCD) have set up what is believed to be the first data link from a K–12 school to a major university in the state of California. This data link connects DSHS's computer lab to UCD's computer network and affords access to a wide variety of data available through UCD's Internet connection. It has allowed the high school to expand its computer studies curriculum, thus opening new horizons for students interested in computer applications and research. It is also providing opportunities for innovative teaching and work methods for students and faculty in all the other departments at DSHS.

Pacific Bell's intention is to help the University of California system and the State University system to fulfill their commitments to the community by using telecommunications to support the educational process at elementary, junior high and high schools. Their vision of the future includes "distance learning" (learning in remote classrooms linked to larger schools or universities), use of electronic messaging systems by parents and school personnel as well as students, and increased opportunities for multilingual students, those with disabilities and those who need alternate approaches.

The University of California, Davis is heavily involved in computer network research and actively participates in international network standards committees. Computer networks are becoming an increasingly important utility, particularly in the academic and research communities. UCD is currently connected to all three of the major international networks that are used for educational and research information exchange, plus BARRNet (Bay Area Regional Research Network) and NSFNET (National Science Foundation Network).

Davis Senior High School in Davis, California, is the largest campus in the Davis Joint Unified School District, with an enrollment of over 1,100 students. It is a comprehensive high school. The school district has strong community support, but limited resources.

A 56 kilobit per second Advanced Digital Network (ADN) circuit is the data link from Davis Senior High School to the UC Davis campus. This service provides high quality digital transmission as well as variable data speeds, error detection, and flexible expansion for growth. Lines have been set from the present (12 computer) network and its server to the library and those computers are connected to the local network. Future plans include lines out to classrooms in anticipation of placement of computers in these areas. Apple Corporation has provided the high school with a new network server (a Macintosh IICX) with additional hardware and software to support the local area network. They have also provided computers for additional classroom stations and two CD-ROM players.

The first two groups of teachers and students have been trained, and the reception has been enthusiastic. The teachers are so enthusiastic that some of them have devoted one of their vacation days during winter break to a workshop to familiarize themselves with network use. A significant number of students and teachers are using MELVYL™ for library research assistance. Several classes have used the information stored on Compact Disc (CD) databases for classroom reports. Because of the ease of use (and perhaps the novelty), students constantly browse through the CDs we now own (a history database, a database with information on various countries, a CD containing public domain software and several CDs containing programming information).

Teachers are using the network to do research and use electronic mail systems. They can communicate with other teachers and authorities in specialized fields, and use outside databases as sources of new information for classroom support. One teacher, Cliff Simes, has already begun his own search for resources and has found an additional bulletin board to use--one devoted to teachers in the Vocational Education field (CAVIX).

Teachers are able to communicate with professional organizations over Internet (including the Modern Language Association, American Association of Teachers of Spanish and Portuguese, Association of Teachers of French, American Association of Teachers of German, American Association of Teachers of Mathematics, etc.). They can also download public domain software from database software collections to support instruction and aid in classroom management.

Both students and teachers have access to UCD's newsgroups, which provide articles and opportunities for discussion of many subjects, ranging from "Applications of Artificial Intelligence to Education" to postings for many types of computers, general news, and a variety of cultural and academic topics. It is planned that there will be a small "talk area" set aside specifically for topics initiated by teachers at DSHS (for example, questions open for discussion in the various foreign languages taught at the school). Other plans include possible correspondence with students in other countries and in other parts of the United States.

Some students have already joined the "talk groups" on UCD's network and have read and responded to articles on topics from aeronautics and physics to discussions of the Middle East, "C" language for the computer and recent political events. One of the chief attractions of this type of communication is that the students are seen as equal participants in the communication process, not as "kids" playing with the computers. Their comments must be carefully thought out and are given equal weight with messages from the other members of the discussion. This promotes a form of "electronic democracy," one of the themes in which Pacific Bell has shown strong interest.

Beginning in September 1990, teachers and students will use the network for immediate classroom access to information to be used in discussions and projects (e.g. backup statistics, news items, electronic mail to other classes). They will use network support in classroom discussions and to support individual or small–group cooperative work in classroom settings.

Have there been any problems? Not yet. Joan Gargano and Russell Hobby of UCD have provided the high school with a guide to network etiquette and guides for the many facets of telecommunications. Staff at the UC Davis library have provided us with guides to MELVYL™. Everyone at the school who has access to the network has read the documents and has promised to follow the guidelines. They know that even with the grant and expertise from Pacific Bell, the machines from Apple, and the help from the Internet Federation and UCD, responsibility for the success of this project rests with the students and faculty at the high school.

Janet Meizel is a teacher at Davis Senior High School, Davis, California, and a lecturer at the University of California, Davis School of Medicine; Internet: jemeizel@ucdavis.edu.

"Free-Netting"

The Development of Free. Public Access Community Computer Systems

T.M. Grundner, Ed.D

National Public Telecomputing Network

For the past 20 years futurists have been making a common prediction. Someday, we are told, everyone will be able to use computers to send electronic mail across town or around the world, access medical and legal information, find out what's going on at their children's schools, complain to the mayor about the potholes, access the local public library card catalog, and so forth, all without ever leaving the comfort of home.

For some that vision has become reality via one or more of the many commercial videotex companies which now exist. But the high cost of those commercial services have, in general, prevented most average citizens from using them. The result has been an "Information Age" which is becoming populated more by people with $50,000+ household incomes than anyone else.

For the past five years researchers at Case Western Reserve University in Cleveland, Ohio have been working on the development of extremely cost-efficient methods of delivering community based computerized information and communications services. Their work has resulted in a system which is so inexpensive to operate that it can be provided by virtually any community as a free public service.

This report will touch on two aspects of their work. The first is the development of the Cleveland Free-Net™, a prototype community computer system which currently averages about 2,000 logins a day and provides over 125 information and communications services to the Cleveland area. The second is the development of the National Public Telecomputing Network, a nonprofit organization devoted to disseminating this technology to other cities and linking them together into a common network.

Because of space limitations, the following will only briefly outline these developments. Those wishing more information may contact the author at addresses shown at the end of the article.

The Cleveland Free-Net™ [1]

The Cleveland Free-Net™ is a free, open-access, community computer system operated by Case Western Reserve University. Established in July 1986, the central Free-Net™ [2] computer has been programmed to allow anyone with a home, office, or school computer and a device called a modem, to call in 24 hours a day and access a wide range of electronic services and features. These services range from free world-wide electronic mail, to information in areas such as health, education, technology, government, arts, recreation, and the law.

The key to the economics of operating a Free-Net™ is the fact that the system is literally run by the community itself. Every feature that appears on the system is there because of individuals or organizations in the community who contribute their time, effort, and expertise to bring it online and operate it. On the Cleveland Free-Net™, for example, there are over 250 "sysops" (system operators) who are doctors, lawyers, educators, community group representatives, hobbyists, etc. each operating their own area and, thereby, contributing to the electronic whole. This is in contrast to the commercial systems which have very high personnel and information-acquisition costs and must pass those costs on to the consumer.

[1]. To view the Cleveland Free-Net™ system have your modem dial (216) 368-3888 (300/1200/2400 baud).

[2]. Free-Net™ and Cybercasting™ are registered servicemarks of the National Public Telecomputing Network.

The first version of the Free-Net™ attracted over 7,000 registered users and averaged between 500 and 600 calls a day on ten incoming phone lines. In August 1989 Free-Net™ II opened and currently averages over 2,000 logins a day on 48 telephone lines. At the moment the Free-Net™ has a user base of about 10,000 persons, which is expected to grow eventually to at least 15–20,000 registered users in the Cleveland area. Eighty-six percent of Free-Net™ users are over the age of twenty (average age 35.5 years) with a very deep middle class socio-economic penetration.

Inherent in the project from the beginning was the idea that, if we were successful, we would make every attempt to disseminate this technology to other cities. As a result, in September 1989 the National Public Telecomputing Network was born.

The National Public Telecomputing Network (NPTN)

The concept behind NPTN is not new. You are probably familiar with National Public Radio and Public Broadcasting on television. To understand NPTN, simply substitute community computer systems for radio or television stations, and you have the core of what the organization hopes to accomplish.

NPTN is a nonprofit corporation which is funded completely by voluntary membership dues from the users of its community computer systems, corporate and foundation grants and donations, and other fund-raising activities.

One of its main objectives is to establish as many community computer systems as possible throughout the country. To that end the necessary software is being made available to qualified parties, on a license basis, for $1 a year. Each Free-Net™ system is an affiliate of NPTN, which provides inter-system electronic mail handling and other services. In addition, NPTN provides Cybercasting™ services whereby a wide variety of quality news and information features are delivered to the affiliates via NPTN feed — a concept very similar to that of any radio or television broadcasting network. A five city network of NPTN community computers currently exists, with more expected to come online later this year.

Services

The list of services available on any given Free-Net™ is limited only by the resources of the community in which it operates. The Cleveland system, for example, has 16 "buildings" which cover areas such as: government, the arts, science and technology, education, medicine, recreation, libraries, community affairs, business and industry, and law. It even has a "Teleport" which will transfer people to other area computer systems such as the Cleveland Public Library and other major libraries throughout northeast Ohio, and a "post office" to provide free electronic mail.

NPTN network services include such features as: national and international electronic mail via the Internet, the dissemination of U.S. Supreme Court opinions within minutes of their release, the "Congressional Memory Project" which provides summaries of House and Senate bills and how our congresspersons voted on them, and hopefully soon, will be providing a network-wide electronic news service.

The Greening of a Medium

Toward the end of the last century the public library as we know it today did not exist. Eventually, however, literacy became high enough (and the cost of books cheap enough) that the free public library became feasible. People in cities and towns all over the country got together to make free public access to the printed word a reality. The result was a legacy from which virtually everyone reading this document has, at one point or another, benefited.

We believe we have reached a point in this century where computer "literacy" has gotten high enough (and the cost of the equipment low enough) that a demand for free, public access, computerized information systems has developed.

The Cleveland Free-Net™ proved it could be done. NPTN is currently about the business of establishing these systems in cities throughout the country. And the futuristic dream of universal information and communication services for the community — all of the community — is not that far from becoming a reality.

For more information about the Cleveland Free-Net™ or NPTN, please contack: T.M. Grundner, Ed.D., President, NPTN, Box 1987, Cleveland, OH 44106; Voice: (216) 368-2733; FAX: (216) 368-5436; Internet: aa001@cleveland.freenet.edu.

LITA Discussion Paper

Developing the Information Superhighway
Issues for Libraries

EDWIN BROWNRIGG, PH.D.

The Memex Research Institute

This paper was commissioned by the Library and Information Technology Association, a division of the American Library Association, to provide a basis for discussion of library participation in current efforts to establish a national telecommunications "superhighway". The paper outlines the convergence of library automation and educational networking, and relates the importance of recent trends to future library service. The impact of the existing higher education network (Internet) and the proposed National Research and Education Network (NREN) on library service is explored. Public policy issues are defined, including the availability of resources, access to the resources, definition and adherence to standards, and boundary problems. To support the needed debate on public policy issues, ten principles for operation of publicly supported networking, within and beyond the NREN, are proposed.

We live in an era of change in modes of communication [1]. At the root of our social changes, and our legal reactions to them, is a key technological change: communication, other than face–to–face, is becoming overwhelmingly electronic. Not only is electronic communication growing faster than communication through the traditional medium of print, but also the convergence of the modes of delivery (print, common carriage, and broadcasting) is bringing newspapers, journals, and books to the threshold of digital electronic communication.

By the late 1970s, broadcasting had grown to the point where, on the average, Americans consumed four times as many words electronically as they read in print [2]. Yet, at the same time, publication of printed material was growing annually at a rate of five percent. Then through the 1980s, academics and business people came to embrace electronic mail and telefacsimile through common carriers as electro–typographic means of personal expression.

Along the arrow of time of human communications, our era is a mere speck compared to the preceding stretches. The arrow began with a long tail of communication by sound. That was followed by a stretch of communication by writing, and then by a stub of communication by print. At the tip of the arrow is the speck of our era of electronic communication. Understandably, our laws and public policies look back on the arrow of time for past analogies as we

try to move ahead. From time to time it makes sense to revisit aging laws applied to then "new" communication modes of the past. The advent of a national network for research and education is such an occasion, and has prompted the commissioning of this work.

In the past our various modes of communication were separate from each other, and the enterprises built upon them similarly distinct. Newspaper publishers and phonograph record producers, for example, did not get in each other's way. But today the historically separate modes of communication are converging due to the adroitness of digital electronics. Voice, music, text, images, motion video, numerical data, and computer programs, are all in the domain of digital electronics. By means of digital electronics they can all be created, collected, organized, distributed, reorganized, copied, displayed or performed.

These activities for handling the various modes of communication are library functions. And, most significantly, all of these heretofore separate modes of communication can now play across the same electronic network.

There can be little wonder at the confusion reflected both in our reactive laws for new communications technologies, and in the public policies for future priorities, practices, and rights in communication.

The Convergence of Libraries and Networking

The library profession stepped toward the threshold of digital electronic communication by perfecting the MARC cataloging communication standard over twenty years ago. At almost the same time, on the other side of Washington, D.C., plans for the ARPANET were developing. A decade later, and without precedent, the Division of Library Automation at the University of California created subnet 31 of the ARPA Internet in order to make available nationwide, MARC–based bibliographic data from the MELVYL™ online union catalog.

Now a growing number of library catalogs are appearing on the same nationwide network (the Internet) that has come to form the basis for the proposed National Research and Education Network (NREN).

There is good reason that libraries should connect to the NREN. Common to those in the professions of computing, communications, and libraries has been the experience that when communities of people are surveyed as to how they would use an electronic network were one provided to them, the most frequent response (usually greater than the others combined) is:

I would access library services.

But librarians, who have traditionally dealt primarily with the separate mode of print, may not have been fully prepared for the implications of such a perception on the part of the patron/user. Nonetheless, the NREN is soon likely to become real after twenty years of tough decisions, public funding, institutional funding, and experimentation at campuses, laboratories, computer centers, research institutes, archives, and libraries. It falls to this generation of librarians to relate library services to network users' expectations.

The National Research and Education Network (NREN)

What is now being proposed under the name "National Research and Education Network" started in 1969 as an experiment under the sponsorship of the United States Advanced Research Projects Agency (ARPA), an agency of the Department of Defense. The intent was to connect a small number of heterogeneous and geographically dispersed computers for the purpose of gaining experience in techniques for providing remote login access from one computer to another or through a series of intermediate computers. The first practical application of the experiment, although not originally a planned one, was electronic mail.

The core of the design of the experiment was a small computer that would act as a switch to route packets of data back and forth among their sources and destinations. The model for the design was similar to the way the telephone network operates. Each computer was like a telephone connected to a local switch from which all other computers could be contacted. In addition, significant improvements over the telephone model were introduced into the ARPANET packet switching scheme.

Since one of the primary goals of the network architecture was overall network survivability, the packet switches were designed to switch from one circuit to another in the event that any given circuit became congested or was interrupted. Another novelty was the introduction of a suite of protocols that could be programmed into computers connected to the ARPANET. These protocols would make it possible to transmit packets over a network composed of diverse physical media and circuits of different bit rates. By the 1980s, these protocols had evolved and allowed multiple and diverse networks to be connected to each other and thus to provide end–to–end service across many different networks. These mature protocols were called Transmission Control Protocol and Internet Protocol (TCP/IP).

Perhaps the single most important realization of the ARPANET by the mid–1970s was that a community of different computers and operating systems could communicate with each other. At first the ARPANET grew slowly, but in the 1970s it added one new computer every twenty days. By the early 1980s the ARPANET was acquiring an increasing number of military sites, and it became clear that for security purposes there would have to be a split between research and military use. Thus MILNET (the military network) was created and diverged from ARPANET. This was a tribute to the success of the ARPANET, but it also called into question how ARPANET's future would be funded, once the Defense Department had gone its separate networking way.

After the split, the name "Internet" entered the community's vocabulary for the network referent. Grave concerns grew over the funding issue, and various schemes were advanced for "managing" the Internet. Fortunately for the Internet community, in the early 1980s the National Science Foundation (NSF) had elevated supercomputing to a national science priority. Five supercomputer centers were established around the United States, and NSF funded further growth and expansion of the Internet as a means of enabling users remote from any of the five supercomputing sites to have access to supercomputing. The challenge then was to increase dramatically the speed of the network from a maximum speed of 56 kilobits per second to 1.5 megabits per second. Many in the community felt that this 28–fold increase in network speed would defeat the TCP/IP protocols, but this proved false, and now some NREN proponents are lobbying for speeds from 3 to 5 gigabits per second by the year 2000. If such speeds are realized, then NREN will be the *de facto* "information highway" envisioned by Senator Albert Gore, Jr.

Two chief issues arise from the information highway scenario. First, which information services will use the NREN? Second, how will the NREN be financed? As of March 1990 these issues were still open. At the National Net'90 Conference, the formation of the Coalition for Networked Information was announced. Sponsored by the Association of Research Libraries (ARL), EDUCOM, and CAUSE, the Coalition is setting an agenda from which to discuss these two major issues and the many others that will arise in developing the NREN.

Kenneth M. King, president of EDUCOM, originally described his vision of a networked scholarly community on December 8, 1988, at a joint meeting of the Library of Congress Network Advisory Committee and the EDUCOM Networking and Telecommunications Task Force. His vision embodied four objectives:

• Connect every scholar in the world to every other scholar and thus reduce the barriers to scholarly interaction of space, time, and cultures.

• Connect to the network all important information sources, specialized instruments, and computing resources worth sharing.

• Build databases that are collaboratively and dynamically maintained that contain all that is known on a particular subject.

• Create a knowledge management system on the network that will enable scholars to navigate through these resources in a standard, intuitive, and consistent way.

The latter two objectives are fundamental library functions and the second (connecting to the network all important information sources) could be a library function in the future.

Funding for the NREN

The Coalition for the National Research and Education Network (not to be confused with the ARL/EDUCOM/CAUSE Coalition above) was formed to articulate the network challenge, to describe the NREN's benefits and beneficiaries, to propose a plan for the NREN's growth, to focus the issue of its funding and by whom, and to propose next steps.

In its 1989 brochure entitled *NREN: The National Research and Education Network* the Coalition proposes that

... the Network will give researchers and students at colleges of all sizes — and at large and small companies — in every state access to the same:

- high performance computing tools

- data banks

- supercomputers

- libraries

- specialized research facilities

- educational technology

that are presently available to only a few large universities and laboratories that can afford them.

From this one can infer that the proponents of the NREN have a pluralistic approach.

The Coalition for the NREN declares that federal funding is critically needed to:

• stimulate the additional investments needed at the local and regional level; and

• provide an infrastructure that will bring the benefits of those local and regional investments to the entire nation.

There can be little doubt that there are economic advantages in building electronic networks, because campus after campus, and region after region, have done so. A proposal for $400 million for the NREN is currently before Congress as an initial request for 1991 through 1995. The Coalition for the NREN proposes that campuses continue to contribute to the cost of building local networks that would attach to the NREN, and that telecommunications companies contribute to the research and development of technologies that would enhance the speed and quality of services on the NREN.

One of the basic problems with the issue of funding the NREN is that most of the organizations connected to the Internet currently pay for the leased telecommunications circuits that link them to an Internet gateway. To add to the confusion, some of the long high–speed circuits in the Internet are underwritten by their common carriers. These practices may give rise to the appearance that, in large part, the proposed NREN would start as self–funding and, thus, not be in need of public support. The EDUCOM Networking and Telecommunications Task Force (NTTF) addresses this perception and reports in its *Policy Paper* revised March 1990 that "[t]he federal government, through its research sponsoring agencies, has historically been the major source of funding for inter–campus network facilities, with the current level estimated at $50 million per year."

The issue of cost recovery is also addressed in the EDUCOM NTTF *Policy Paper* that concludes: "Until a useful and detailed accounting procedure is available, the present ... fixed fee basis is considered a fair method of financing the network."

In addition to new federal policies, new federal dollars likely will be required to sustain a national network that will meet the needs of American education and research. Because the amount of new federal dollars available to the NREN will be directly proportional to supportive votes from the citizenry, it may be a fitting strategy to introduce library and information services into the NREN proposal, as they traditionally have enjoyed public tax support at the local and state levels. In addition, since 1966, federal library programs have promoted interlibrary cooperation and resource sharing among all types of libraries through library networks operating across geographic and political boundaries.

In order to achieve the NREN's vision and realize its goals through new policies and new public funding, interested parties need to be clear on these issues (whose resolutions are beyond this paper's scope):

- the domain in which the policy operates

- availability of resources

- organization of access to the resources

- establishment and adherence to standard practices

- problems at NREN's boundaries

NREN Policy and Governance

Governance is perhaps the most daunting aspect of the NREN. During its incarnation as the ARPANET, there was no doubt that the Defense Communication Agency was the maker and enforcer of policy for the network. After the ARPANET/MILNET split, the Internet community was left with a loosely organized community of users whose interrelationships were informal. As a result, different regional networks within the Internet have different policies; different backbone agencies have different policies. NSF has a policy. The Federation of American Research Networks (FARNET) recently issued a usage policy statement. These all differ in some respects.

There are several special interest groups involving themselves in the discussion of policy for the NREN. These range from members of Congress to university administrators, computer center directors, common carrier executives, and librarians.

In addition, publishers are asking for a role in developing a national digital library. A March 15, 1990, press release from the Association of American Publishers, Inc. (AAP) quotes Timothy B. King, vice president of John Wiley & Son as testifying on behalf of AAP to a subcommittee on the House Science, Space and Technology Committee on H.R. 3131 that the best way of protecting scientific publishers' copyright and literature "is to involve us from the beginning," as a "valuable source of information for the network's designers and an active participant in the development of its information infrastructure."

Privacy

How will network security be achieved? Security violations of the Internet are known to have taken place. For the library profession, one issue will be how to achieve a balance between open access and privacy/security? Assuming a resolution of this issue, then, with the cooperation of users, basic information about collection use could be gathered and analyzed. Such data could be valuable for cooperative collection development.

Potential NREN Resources

The agglutination of resources within the Internet is truly impressive. The number of computers connected to the network is in the tens of thousands, and is perhaps in the hundreds of thousands when unknown numbers of personal computers on local networks are taken into account. The major applications among these devices have been electronic mail and other forms of file sharing. Now there are supercomputers on the network, and their services are highly rationed. However, what the community now appears to want in growing demand is more library–like services. This demand represents an evolutionary step beyond electronic information provision taking place within libraries today.

Library–like services are different from traditional library services. Such services reduce to electronics and can emanate remotely from the library. Online catalog and other database access has already begun. So, the challenge for traditional librarians is to readjust further the professional focus from communication primarily by print to communication in significant part by electronics.

Library Online Catalogs on the Proposed NREN

Traditionally, libraries have tightly controlled access by patrons. The methods have been straightforward: open or close the library building's doors, open or close the stacks, adjudicate and enforce book circulation, develop the collection as functions of perceived usership and budget limitations, and provide some form of bibliography to users.

Clearly, as a result of activity on the Internet, users' expectations towards libraries are changing. Although the percentage of libraries whose online catalogs are available on the Internet is small, the implications are great. The most significant implication is that connecting an online catalog to a national network effectively begs the question of open access

to everyone. So far, open access has been the policy of the pioneering libraries who have connected to the Internet.

Standards Practices Within the proposed NREN

ARPANET, the Internet, and now the proposed NREN, as manifestations of the same development, share a history of over twenty years. That only a handful of libraries have incorporated the network into their operations suggests that the continuing convergence of networking and library practices may take a long time. For example, in the name of sound business practices some cataloging utilities continue not to use the Internet, while some vendors of library automation systems have acknowledged the importance of networking protocols.

The issue here is not that standards for libraries' use of the proposed NREN do not exist. To the contrary, communications standards abound within the library community. The NISO Z.39 protocols have been designed to work with the lower layers of the OSI protocols. Arguably, the library profession is a relatively well prepared group to join the Internet community with respect to standards. The issue is that the Internet community does not yet run the OSI protocols, and, therefore, the library profession per force will be involved in a migration from TCP/IP to OSI (Open System Interconnect) on the Internet.

Problems at NREN's Boundaries

There are many who would cite the Internet as being a good example of bad management. At the same time, most of those same people are members of institutions connected in one way or another to the Internet, and many of them use it on a regular basis, if only to exchange electronic mail. For example, defining the line of demarcation between research and education is one of the management problems with the proposed NREN. It arises because of the formal and informal hierarchies within the Internet with respect to both its use and content. As long as priorities are clear, the EDUCOM NTTF approach, to be inclusive rather than exclusive, appears to prevail, provided that it does not erode the value of the network for the very highest quality of research.

Another common attitude toward the Internet has been that it should not carry commercial traffic, although this is changing. This proscription would impede libraries from using the proposed NREN to its fullest potential. The dichotomy has been that the proponents of the NREN have focused mainly on themes of universal access by everyone to everything in the research and education community.

For libraries, universal accessibility would be meaningless without published works. Published works are commercial property. Published works comprise the main content of libraries. Copyright law prohibits unlicensed use of published works across a network, as such use would be an infringement of the copyright holders' display rights. There is a fundamental problem for libraries in using the proposed NREN as the carrier for electronic library services without a resolution of the issue of commercial traffic. A solution to the separate problem of how copyright through the NREN could be handled is addressed in principle TEN below.

The norms of use of the proposed NREN arise not out of law, but out of convention. The resolution of the issue of commercial traffic over the proposed NREN could be an opportunity for libraries to meaningfully influence NREN's countenance and at the same time test the copyright arrangement among publishers, libraries, and the research and education community.

Public Policy Issues for Libraries

Americans today enjoy virtually universal access to the common carrier services of mail, telegraph, and telephone. The same is true for the broadcast services of radio and television. While these services have been universal, the amount and type of content have been limited. Normal telephone service is limited to two-way voice communication. The analog-to-digital conversion of telephone service is limited to 9600 bits per second, roughly the speed at which telegrams have traveled. Broadcast access, though of relatively high capacity in the case of television, is usually only one-way.

As access to computing on campuses has approached universality over the last two decades, the inadequacies of common carrier and broadcasting services have been overcome with local and wide-area networks. Advances in campus networks and regional networks have paralleled those of the national network, but to date, there has been an absence of counterpart private sector services. This suggests the viability of a "public good" approach to developing America's information highway, similar to our "public good" approaches to dealing with goods such as the environment and the electromagnetic spectrum. Using radio spectrum to extend the network to rural campuses is an example of this approach (and is expanded in principle NINE below). It is the same public good approach from which the interstate highway system evolved.

If the NREN is developed as a public good according to the principles listed below, then Americans could access printed information converted to or created in electronic form and delivered via the NREN through their local libraries. Today a local call from home via common carrier to the local library at 9600 bits per second could extend service from the library into the home. If in the future the Federal Communications Commission (FCC) rules change, as per principle NINE below, then a high-speed, shared-channel connection between the home and the local library would be feasible.

With this policy template in mind, a set of principles is hereby put forward for consideration with respect to the NREN. There is a rich scholarship on public policy within America from which to draw to develop such principles. A fitting culmination of such scholarship rests with the late Ithiel de Sola Pool, who in his work, *Technologies of Freedom* (1983), idealized a network of which the NREN is suggestive. There he framed a set of ideal principles that are adapted here for the proposed National Research and Education Network.

Ten Suggested Principles for a National Research and Education Network

The FIRST principle is that the First Amendment apply to all media in the NREN, that is, to the function of communication, not to the medium of communication [3]. That "Congress shall make no law ... abridging freedom of speech or of the press" must apply to communication by digital electronics within the NREN equally as to communication by printing in education and research.

The SECOND principle, following from the FIRST, is that through the NREN anyone may publish at will, with no prior restraint, no licensing, no taxation, and no scrutiny of content by any party [4].

The THIRD principle is that enforcement of the laws and policies of the NREN be after the fact, not by prior review [5].

The FOURTH principle is that the NREN should be enabled as a free market. If it fails as a free market and, therefore, needs to be monopolistic, then apply common carrier regulation rather than direct regulation or public ownership [6].

The FIFTH principle is that of universal interconnection (implying adherence to the standards [7] of TCP/IP as they evolve to those of OSI) and to a firm recognition of the basic right to interconnect. The EDUCOM NTTF has proposed to bound "universal interconnection" within a community composed of universities, government research labs, industrial research labs, national databases, and libraries, as per its NREN brochure.

The SIXTH principle would oblige users, both institutional and individual, to disclose their amount of use [8] of the NREN. This is essential for monitoring and for planning network performance.

The SEVENTH principle is that government and common carriers should be blind to circuit use. What the NREN is used for and how it is used are not their concerns [9]

The EIGHTH principle is that bottlenecks should not be used as a rationale to extend control [10]. As bottlenecks occur, the NREN participants should be left alone to eliminate them by whatever pluralistic process is available, or to live with the consequences of not doing so. The TCP/IP protocols from which the NREN protocols have evolved defy control in the classical management sense, and rest, rather, on the philosophically pluralistic notions of convention, cooperation, interoperability, and redundancy.

The NINTH principle is that regulation of the electromagnetic spectrum for education and research should be separated from regulation extant for interstate commerce [11]. In particular, there remain vast interstices in the rural parts of the NREN that threaten to leave divided the communities of research and education into groups of "haves" and "have–nots." This latter group of "have–nots" is a population of "lone users" who remain unconnected, or inadequately connected, to the NREN.

A publicly funded study needs to be done of the causes and cures of the problem, embodied in Title 47 of the Code of Federal Regulations: Telecommunica-

tion, that limits library access to communications bandwidth. The study must result in an appropriate and effective rules change process within the FCC that, in turn, would enable re–regulation of spectrum that the FCC has already generously set aside for education. The outcome should be a timely use for the NREN of a sliver of the electromagnetic spectrum, a public good, for library services, a public good, for which precedent exists.

The TENTH principle is that intellectual property must be recognized in the NREN. This means that copyright enforcement and royalty distribution must be adapted [12] to the NREN. Perhaps a recasting of ASCAP (American Society of Composers, Authors, and Publishers) or some other remedy is in order, but failing this principle will doom the NREN as a publishing medium. It was the scholarly community that created information publishers, and it has been the published work that libraries collect, organize, preserve and disseminate. A new communications medium must accommodate these traditions and relationships for publishers to accept it.

Future Prospects for Libraries and the NREN

Already in a spirit of cooperation for which the Internet was intended, library users and librarians have discovered benefits from connecting online public access catalogs to the Internet. During the 1980s the Linked Systems Protocol standard evolved and is now ready to be used to allow libraries to share cataloging information with relative ease. Privately funded research continues with LSP (Linked Systems Protocol, NISO Z39.50).

Other types of information resources expected to be available on the NREN are demonstrated by the following projects reported in the *Proposal for an ARL/CAUSE/EDUCOM Coalition for Networked Information.*

• The Medieval Early Modern Data Bank (MEMDB), created by scholars at Rutgers University and made accessible electronically by The Research Libraries Group (RLG)

• Research in Progress (an RLG/RLIN Special Data Base), a file of entries and abstracts of journal articles accepted by but not yet published in several journals indexed by the Modern Language Association, as well as a number of women's studies journals

- A publishing project currently underway at Johns Hopkins University Medical Library in which a database of research findings is available for access by readers, students, and critics who respond directly via electronic mail to the author

- The Geographic Reference Information Network (proposed by RLG), a digitized data file of satellite imagery and geographic information developed by researchers at the University of California, Santa Barbara, working with a number of agencies including the National Center for Geographic Information and NASA

One of the most profound consequences of the NREN for librarians, library users, and the general education and research community is the "virtual library." As described by Richard Goodram [13].

> The most complex information element within any University is the library system. As such it demands special analysis and provides the opportunities for substantial benefits from improvements in its operation. ... The virtual library [combines] an on-site collection of current and heavily used materials, in both print and electronic form, with an electronic network which provides access to, and delivery from, external information sources, library and commercial, worldwide. The design goal for the user is to create the effect of an indefinitely large collection through the electronic access and delivery of materials as needed rather than by expending staff and acquisition funds in an attempt to anticipate future demands for a wide range of retrospective materials and peripheral publications.

Discussions are under way to create a consortium of public libraries which would use the NREN to connect their online catalogs. The purpose of this cooperation would be to enable the "universal borrowing card" so that library users in America's mobile society could move from public library to public library and use each as if it were the same library. Collections so united would be richer and more accessible than that of the Library of Congress.

Finally, if the public policies and laws of the NREN are framed as proposed above, then a currently reluctant publishing sector might more readily strive and cooperate with libraries to perfect the standards still lacking in library practices to describe the composition of editions of works published as digital electronic artifacts. In that way such works could be distributed or copied across the NREN and the copyright owner could receive a fair royalty. Once perfected, such publishing practices should achieve new economies and profits, on the basis that the kinetic energy used in electronic publishing is several orders of magnitude less than that of print publishing.

New standards such as those discussed herein could then be harnessed by governmental agencies for internal communications as well as for communications with the citizens participating in research and education, including citizens who use public libraries.

Conclusion

Adoption of the above proposed ten principles into law and public policy is in significant parts without precedent in American communications. In the beginning, the style of practice of librarianship in America, too, was without precedent, but was rooted in a philosophy of pluralism consistent with the principles suggested herein.

References

[1] *Communications* is from the latin *communicare*, meaning "to make common." With the greek prefix *tele*, meaning "distant", *telecommunications* means "to make common at a distance."

[2] Ithiel de Sola Pool. *Technologies of Freedom* (Cambridge, Mass: Belknap Press, 1984), p. 21.

[3] Ibid., p.235 note 32.

[4] Ibid., p.246.

[5] Ibid.

[6] Ibid.

[7] Ibid.

[8] Ibid., p.248-9.

[9] Ibid.

[10] Ibid.

[11] Ibid., p.249.

[12] Edwin Brownrigg with Brett Butler. *Cooperative Library Networks: Changing the Rules* (Memex Research Institute White Paper #1. California State University, Chico, 1990), p.10.

[13] Richard J. Goodram. *The Virtual Library: Collections on Demand* (Memex Research Institute White Paper #2. California State University, Chico, 1990), p.1.

_____

The opinions expressed in this paper are those of the author. Dr. Edwin Brownrigg is director of research, The Memex Research Institute, 422 Bonita Avenue, Roseville, CA 95678.

Bibliography

Research and Education Networking

A Bibliography

COMPILED BY MARA SAULE

University of Vermont

Little has been published about the uses of research and professional communication networks such as BITNET, Internet, and the proposed NREN, particularly by librarians. Most discussions have dealt with technical aspects of telecommunications networks, or with ethical and copyright issues of network use. The following selective bibliography lists recent articles about telecommunications networks and their implications for libraries, research, and professional communication.

Arms, Caroline, ed. *Campus Networking Strategies*. Bedford, MA: Digital Press, 1988.

Arms, Caroline. "Using the National Networks: BITNET and the Internet." *Online* 14 (September 1990): 24–29.

Avram, Henriette D. "Copyright in the Electronic Environment." *EDUCOM Review* 24,3 (Fall 1989): 31–33.

Bell, C. Gordon. "Gordon Bell Calls for a U.S. Research Network." *IEEE Spectrum* 25 (February 1988): 54–57.

Bell, C. Gordon. "Steps Toward a National Research Telecommunications Network." *Library Hi Tech* 6,1 (1988): 33–36.

Britten, William A. "BITNET and the Internet: Scholarly Networks for Librarians." *College & Research Libraries News* 51,2 (February 1990): 103–107.

Cisler, Steve. "The Library Community and the National Research and Education Network." *Wilson Library Bulletin* 64,10 (June 1990): 51–55.

Cisler, Steve. "NREN: The National Research and Education Network." *LITA Newsletter* 11,2 (Spring 1990): 1–2.

Cline, Nancy. "Information Resources and the National Network." *EDUCOM Review* 25,2 (Summer 1990): 30–34.

Comer, Douglas E. *Internetworking with TCP/IP: Principles, Protocols, and Architecture*. 2nd ed. Englewood Cliffs, NJ: Prentice Hall, 1988.

EDUCOM Bulletin 23,2/3 (Summer/Fall 1988): entire issue.

Frey, Donnalyn and Rick Adams. *A Guide to Electronic Mail Networks and Addressing*. Sebastopol, CA: O'Reilly, 1989.

Gore, Albert. "Remarks on the NREN." *EDUCOM Review* 25,2 (Summer 1990): 12–16.

Huray, Paul G. and David B. Nelson. "The Federal High–Performance Computing Program." *EDUCOM Review* 25,2 (Summer 1990): 17–24.

Jacob, M.E.L. "Libraries and National Library Networks." *Bulletin of the American Society for Information Science* 16,5 (June/July 1990): 8–9.

Kibbey, Mark and Nancy H. Evans. "The Network is the Library." *EDUCOM Review* 24,3 (Fall 1989): 15–20.

Kroll, Ed. *The Hitchhikers Guide to the Internet*. (Available as RFC 1118 by anonymous FTP from NIC.DDN.MIL)

LaQuey, Tracy. "Networks for Academics." *Academic Computing* 4,3 (November 1989): 32–34+.

Learn, Larry L. "Networks: The Telecommunications Infrastructure and Impacts of Change." *Library Hi Tech* 6,1 (1988): 13–27.

Lynch, Clifford A. "The Growth of Computer Networks: A Status Report." *Bulletin of the American Society for Information Science* 16,5 (June/July 1990): 10–11.

Lynch, Clifford A. "Library Automation and the National Research Network." *EDUCOM Review* 24,3 (Fall 1989): 21–26.

Lynch, Clifford A. "Linking Library Automation Systems in the Internet: Functional Requirements, Planning, and Policy Issues." *Library Hi Tech* 7,4 (1989): 7–18.

National Research Network Review Committee, et al. *Toward a National Research Network*. Washington, DC: National Academy Press, 1988. (Available from Computer Science and Technology Board, 2101 Constitution Ave., N.W., Washington, DC 20418.)

Palca, Joseph. "Getting Together Bit by Bit: High–Speed Networks are Growing Like Topsy." *Science* 248 (April 13, 1990): 160–162.

Quarterman, John S. *The Matrix: Computer Networks and Conferencing Systems Worldwide*. Bedford, MA: Digital Press, 1990.

Rogers, Susan M. "Educational Applications of the NREN." *EDUCOM Review* 25,2 (Summer 1990): 25–29.

Schultz, Brad. "The Evolution of ARPANET (Internet)." *Datamation* 34 (August 1, 1988): 71–74. Discussion: Datamation 34 (October 1, 1988): 4.

U.S. Congress, Office of Technology Assessment. *High Performance Computing and Networking for Science––Background Paper*, OTA–BP– CIT–59. Washington, DC: U.S. Government Printing Office, September 1989. (Available from Superintendent of Documents, GPO, Washington, DC 20402-9325; GPO stock number 052–003–01164–6; price $2.25.)

Van Houeling, Douglas E. "The National Network: A National Interest." *EDUCOM Review* 24,2 (Summer 1989): 14–18.

Walsh, John. "Designs on a National Research Network." *Science* 239 (February 19, 1988): 861.

Wintsch, Susan. "Toward a National Research and Education Network." *MOSAIC* 20,4 (Winter 1989): 32–42.

Wright, Karen. "The Road to the Global Village." *Scientific American* 262,3 (March 1990): 83–85+.

Wulf, William A. "Government's Role in the National Network." *EDUCOM Review* 24,2 (Summer 1989): 22–26.

Mara Saule, instruction coordinator at the Bailey/Howe Library, University of Vermont, is currently chair of the LITA Education Committee.

Glossary

Glossary of Terms, Networks, and Organizations

COMPILED BY R. BRUCE MILLER

University of California, San Diego

AAP   Association of American Publishers

Advanced Research Projects Agency (ARPA)   An agency of the Department of Defense

ALA   American Library Association

ALANET   Electronic mail system provided by the American Library Association

American Library Association (ALA)   An organization to provide leadership for the development, promotion, and improvement of library and information services and the profession of librarianship in order to enhance learning and ensure access to information for all

AppleLink   An electronic mail, databank, and bulletin board system for use by employees, dealers, customers, and consultants of Apple Computer, Inc.

ARL   Association of Research Libraries

ARPA   Advanced Research Projects Agency (old name for DARPA)

ARPANET   A wide area network that began as an experiment to connect hosts and terminal servers together; the first packet network on the Internet

ASCAP   American Society of Composers, Authors, and Publishers

ASIA   Asian Shared Information & Access;

Asian Shared Information & Access (ASIA)   Commercial venture to provide machine readable catalog records for Asian language materials

Association of Research Libraries (ARL)   A group of more than 100 university, public, private, and national research libraries working together to strengthen research library resources and services

BARRNet   Bay Area Regional Research Network; a mid-level component of NSFNET

BITNET   Because It's Time Network; a network connecting academic and research organizations; run by EDU-COM

CARL   Colorado Alliance for Research Libraries

CAUSE (non-acronym)   An association for the management of information technology in higher education

CAVIX   An electronic bulletin board devoted to teachers in the vocational education field

Cleveland Free-Net   see   **Free-Net**

CLSA   California Library Services Act

CNI Coalition for Networked Information

CNREN Coalition for the National Research and Education Network

Coalition for Networked Information (CNI) Formed by the Association of Research Libraries, EDUCOM, and CAUSE to promote the provision of information resources on existing networks and on proposed interconnected networks; not to be confused with the Coalition for the National Research and Education Network

Coalition for the National Research and Education Network (CNREN) Formed to articulate the network challenge, to describe the NREN's benefits and beneficiaries, to propose a plan for the NREN's growth, to focus the issue of its funding and by whom, and to propose the next steps; not to be confused with the Coalition for Networked Information

Colorado Alliance for Research Libraries (CARL) A consortium of academic and public libraries to provide computer based library services

CompuServe An electronic home and business information service provided by CompuServe, Inc.

CSNET Computer and Science Network

Cybercasting A trademarked service of the National Public Telecomputing Network whereby a wide variety of news and information features are delivered to affiliates

DARPA Defense Advanced Research Projects Agency

Davis Senior High School (DSHS) A high school in California involved in an experimental data link with the University of California, Davis

Dialog An online information retrieval service provided by Dialog Information Services, Inc.

Distance learning Learning in remote classrooms or at home via linkage to a remote school or a larger school or university

DSHS Davis (CA) Senior High School

EDUCOM (non–acronym) A coalition of several hundred colleges and universities to promote the use of information technology in higher education

FARNET Federation of American Research Networks

FCC Federal Communications Commission

FCCSET (pronounced "fix it") Federal Coordinating Council for Science, Engineering, and Technology

Federal Networking Council (FNC) Joint U.S. government body which oversees U.S. federal policy on networking

FidoNet Made up mostly of MS/PC–DOS personal computers linked over public dial–up telephone lines

FNC Federal Networking Council

Free–Net A free, open-access, community computer system

Gigabit One billion bits, a measure of quantity of machine encoded data

Internet A sprawling composite of many hundreds of local and wide area networks united by the same transmission protocols and primarily connected by the cross country electronic backbone provided by the NSFNET; it is estimated that far in excess of 100,000 computers are connected to the Internet; usage of the term began following the split of MILNET from ARPANET

Internet Protocol (IP) The set of rules at the network level that controls routing and switching operations that allow different networks to pass data

IP Internet Protocol

LAMA Library Administration and Management Association

LAN Local Area Network

Library Administration and Management Association (LAMA) A division of the American Library Association; provides an organizational framework for encouraging the study of administrative theory, for improving the practice of administration in libraries, and for identifying and fostering administrative skills

Library and Information Technology Association (LITA) A division of the American Library Association; concerned with the planning, development, design, application, and integration of technologies within the library and information environment, with the impact of emerging technologies on library service, and with the effect of automated technologies on people

LITA Library and Information Technology Association

Library without walls The concept of remote access to the contents and services of libraries and other information resources; combines an on-site collection of current and heavily used materials, in both print and electronic form, with an electronic network which provides access to, and delivery from, external worldwide library and commercial information sources; also "virtual library"

Linked Systems Protocol (LSP) Standard for computer to computer communication for bibliographic information retrieval; NISO Z39.50

Local Area Network (LAN) A computer network for a limited geographical area that allows each node to communicate with every other node

LSCA Library Services and Construction Act; funding source for a variety of library related projects

LSP Linked Systems Protocol

MARC MAchine Readable Cataloging; standard for communication of machine readable cataloging data

Medieval Early Modern Data Bank (MEMDB) Created by scholars at Rutgers University to serve as an online reference system; an example of the type of information that can be made available electronically

MEDLINE (non-acronym) Biomedical and health sciences database supported by the National Library of Medicine

MELVYL (non-acronym) Online union catalog of the University of California System

MEMDB Medieval Early Modern Data Bank

Merit Computer Network A consortium of state-supported universities in Michigan; the Merit organization manages the NSFNET

MILNET The military network that resulted from the split for security purposes of the research and military use of ARPANET

NAC Library of Congress Network Advisory Committee

NASA National Air and Space Administration

National Commission on Libraries and Information Science (NCLIS) Advises the President and the Congress on the nation's library and information needs

National digital library Senator Gore's vision of the access to national resources to be provided by NREN; related to the concept of "library without walls" and "virtual library"

National Information Standards Organization (NISO–Z39) Develops and promotes the use of voluntary standards for libraries, the information sciences, and the publishing industries; "Z39" is due to the former name, American National Standards Committee Z39

National Public Telecomputing Network (NPTN) A non-profit organization devoted to disseminating community computer service

National Research and Education Network (NREN) A proposed telecommunications infrastructure which would expand and upgrade the existing interconnected array of research networks

National Science Foundation (NSF) Agency for the support of basic and applied research and education in science and engineering

National Telecommunications and Information Administration (NTIA) An agency of the Commerce Department

NCLIS National Commission on Libraries and Information Science

NISO National Information Standards Organization

NISO–Z39 National Information Standards Organization; "Z39" is due to the former name, American National Standards Committee Z39

NISO Z39.50 Linked Systems Protocol

NPTN National Public Telecomputing Network

NREN National Research and Education Network

NSF National Science Foundation

NSFNET National Science Foundation Network; forms the "backbone" of the Internet

NTIA National Telecommunications and Information Administration

NTTF EDUCOM Networking and Telecommunications Task Force

NYSERNET New York State Education and Research Network; a mid-level component of NSFNET

OCLC Online Computer Library Center A not-for-profit computer library services and research membership organization

Open System Interconnect (OSI) A theoretical framework by which networking issues are separated into primary components that are amenable to standards; an emerging set of standards that presumably will replace the TCP/IP suite of protocols over time

OSI   Open System Interconnect

OSTP   Office of Science and Technology Policy

Research Libraries Group (RLG)   A partnership of major universities and other research institutions dedicated to improving the management of the information resources necessary for the advancement of scholarship

RLG   Research Libraries Group

Research Libraries Information Network (RLIN)   Supports the cooperative efforts of The Research Libraries Group in collection management and development, preservation, shared resources, technical systems, and bibliographic control

RLIN   Research Libraries Information Network

SURANET   Southeastern Universities Research Network; a mid–level component of NSFNET

TCP/IP   Transmission Control Protocol and Internet Protocol

Transmission Control Protocol (TCP)   The set of rules that formats the packaging of data for transmission between computers

UCD   University of California, Davis

UUCP   Unix to Unix Copy Program; a protocol for data communications

University of California, Davis (UCD)   A university involved in an experimental data link with a high school

Virtual library   The concept of remote access to the contents and services of libraries and other information resources; combines an on–site collection of current and heavily used materials, in both print and electronic form, with an electronic network which provides access to, and delivery from, external worldwide library and commercial information sources; also "library without walls"

The WELL   Regional computer teleconference system in the San Francisco area

Z39   see   **National Information Standards Organization**

SOURCES (in addition to the context of the preceding papers):

1988 Encyclopedia of Information Systems and Services. 8th ed. Detroit: Gale, 1988.

Comer, Douglas E. *Internetworking with TCP/IP: Principles, Protocols, and Architecture.* 2nd ed. Englewood Cliffs, NJ: Prentice Hall, 1988.

Frey, Donnalyn and Rick Adams. A *Guide to Electronic Mail Networks and Addressing.* Sebastopol, CA: O'Reilly, 1989.

Wintsch, Susan. "Toward a National Research and Education Network" *Mosaic* 20, No. 4: 32–42 (Winter 1989).

R. Bruce Miller, assistant university librarian – technical services, University of California, San Diego, is on the LITA Board of Directors.